SUSAN MASON'S
SILVER✣SERVICE

SUSAN MASON'S

SILVER ~ SERVICE

SUSAN MASON AND BARRIE SCARDINO

PELICAN PUBLISHING COMPANY
Gretna 2007

First printing, June 2006
Second printing, December 2006
Third printing, March 2007
Fourth printing, July 2007

---

*The word "Pelican" and the depiction of a pelican are trademarks
of Pelican Publishing Company, Inc., and are registered in the
U.S. Patent and Trademark Office.*

ISBN-13: 978-1-58980-379-4

*Photography by Dan Saelinger, assistant Ben Dashwood
Additional photography by Richard Leo Johnson and
    Savannah College of Art and Design photography archives
Cover and book design by Design Press
Copyediting by Andrea Chesman and Kerri O'Hern*

Printed in Korea

Published by Pelican Publishing Company, Inc.
1000 Burmaster Street, Gretna, Louisiana 70053

This is a Design Press book
Design Press is a division of the Savannah College *of* Art *and* Design

This book is dedicated to my mother,
Christine Seay Vestal,
from whom I got my cooking gene.

And to my best friend,
Jane Hancock Long,
who helped me develop it.

WRITING A COOKBOOK WAS NEVER ON MY AGENDA—I AM BUSY ENOUGH PLANNING PARTIES AND COOKING. But when *Savoring Savannah* (2001) was published featuring me among four other Savannah chefs, I was surprised that people began to ask me when my own cookbook was coming out. When Janice Shay, Director of Design Press at the Savannah School of Art and Design (SCAD), approached me with such a possibility, I was definitely interested not just for myself but for my wonderful staff who have contributed greatly to my success: Christine Ragland, Donna Edwards, Greg Williams, Annette Jackson, Barbara Fleetwood, Addie B. Coston, Denise Proctor, Marlyn Sasser, and especially Mary Reeves whose children and grandchildren have also worked for me over the years.

Paula Wallace, President of SCAD, has been a great supporter of mine, and I envy her vision and energy. She has allowed me to stretch and grow in my business and has continually nurtured my creativity.

I also want to thank my close circle of friends who have encouraged me every step of the way and who have been good clients as well as good friends: Helen Downing, Judy Bradley, Ann Tatum, Greg Parker, Cindy Moore, Diana Barrow, Jean Brooks, Cora Bett Thomas, Joan Sumner, Ellen Bolch, and Lorraine Parè. I call Alice Dasher, who works at E. Shaver bookstore, my "cookbook guru." At the drop of a hat she can find a recipe for me, and is indeed a great cook herself.

When Janice asked me to do this book, I knew I could write recipes in my sleep, but I also knew I needed someone else to help me organize my thoughts and get them down on paper. My talented friend and writer Barrie Scardino was perfect for the job; she can't cook, but she can write. We have enjoyed this collaboration and think that together, we have created a great cookbook.

The seventy plus recipes in this book are mine, but many of them are based on ideas from generations of other Southern cooks. As any chef will tell you, we all build on each other's work. Over the twenty plus years in business, I have probably lost track of the origin of some recipes printed here. Thank you to those who are not acknowledged, but on whose foundation my cooking stands. ⸻

Susan Mason
November, 2005

SUSAN MASON IS ONE OF A KIND. Her stylish appearance and sophisticated taste complement her breezy Southern charm. I'd probably want her to do my parties even if she couldn't cook. Her food is, of course, delicious, but when she puts on a party—whether it's a lavish wedding for hundreds or a family oyster roast—everything is perfect. I don't know how many parties she's done for me over the years, but every single one has been just exactly what I asked for and then some. When Susan is your caterer you know you'll get the best of everything, including her own personal style. When I lived in New York, I discovered that so many celebrities and other New Yorkers love her parties because they are so original. She's an artist, always creative about the menu, decorations, and everything else from the lighting to the plates. Her staff is well-trained, and they enjoy working for her because she treats them the same way she treats her celebrity clients. I worry about the day she'll be too busy with parties for the rich and famous to cater for her old friends. ❧

Barrie Scardino
November, 2005

Contents

INTRODUCTION

DELICIOUS AND GORGEOUS ARE THE TWO WORDS I HOPE PEOPLE USE TO DESCRIBE EVERY PARTY I CATER. Entertaining is show business, and I see myself as a director of top-notch, award-winning productions. I am a total perfectionist when it comes to my parties, so I never leave anything to chance. I overbuy and plan for the worst so I always have extra food, extra plates, extra everything. Thank goodness my clients are willing to pay for what I regard as insurance that things will go as expected.

I grew up in Dothan, down in the southeast corner of Alabama, where—to give you a clue—there was a sign at the country club that read "No Pea-Shelling By The Pool." Now this wasn't so far-fetched because we all spent a lot of time shelling peas—English peas, black-eyed peas, pigeon peas, and whatever other kind of peas that grew there. My mother and my grandmother, whom we called "Other Mama," fixed huge dinners in the middle of the day on Saturday and Sunday for hoards of family and friends.

Our family said "I love you" with food. You never knew who would be there for dinner. We always used our sterling silver and good china and had fresh flowers decorating the table. Treasuring and using beautiful things is a Southern tradition I grew up with and value to this day. I really wasn't interested in cooking then, but I was in love with the feeling that came from those gorgeous meals around which so much of the fun and warmth in my life was built.

I have never advertised, but depended on word of mouth to help my business grow. I have eight full-time staff and scores of waiters and bartenders who work parties for me. I stick to the main principles on which I began my business: always use the freshest, best ingredients, have more than enough food, and make everything look wonderful.

Because I plan and excecute everything the old-fashioned way, this cookbook is good for home cooks and people who do their own entertaining. I don't use mandolines or commercial choppers. My kitchen staff is trained to do everything by hand, and that's the way I approach my catering. The result is that no two parties I do are ever alike. ᐟ

GIRLS, GOSSIP, AND GRITS

ALL MY PARTIES BEGIN WHEN I INVITE THE CLIENT TO MY HOME
FOR LUNCH, NOT FOR A TASTING MENU—BECAUSE I NEVER DO
THAT—BUT BECAUSE I LIKE TO PLAN EVERYTHING OVER FOOD.
I have formed many treasured friendships at my table planning important events. Many of
my clients know each other. Since I've been catering in Savannah for over twenty years, new
people hire me because they know I have a sense of how Savannah likes to do things.

I learned a valuable lesson about entertaining from Craig Claiborne—and it isn't about
food. I bumped into him in the Hamptons, and he invited my mother, my sisters, and me to
his home. When we got there, we were surprised to find his whole house filled with round
tables. We looked around with quizzical expressions, so he explained, "When I entertain, I
always put people at round tables because a round table generates wonderful conversation."
I came right home and got two big round tables that I still have in my front rooms. When I
have my clients over, we sit at one of those round tables; we talk, we look at my portfolio, and then
I go in for the kill and give them a wonderful lunch and a good glass of wine. I prepare an easy
menu because I don't want to be jumping up and down—usually shrimp salad in hot weather
and my world-famous chicken pot pie when it's cold outside. I change menus according to
the season not only because different fresh fruits and vegetables are available different times

of year, but also because the mood and feeling of the food is equally important. No one in Savannah wants steaming oyster stew in the summer or cold cucumber soup in winter. I usually have the job by the time the client leaves my house. More deals are made over good food than in the boardroom.

Even if they are in their eighties, Southern women call each other girls. A great example of our support for each other happened last summer. One of my friends discovered a little jewel box of a store on Madison Avenue

in New York. She dragged all seven of us girls, who were there together for a little R and R, into this store to try on jewelry. Every time one of us put on something, we'd all ooh and ahh and say, "You have to have that necklace, it will go perfectly with your green suit," or "Those earrings match your eyes, you must get them!" Finally the woman who was running the store said, "I've never seen anything like you. Most women who come in here with friends say to each other, 'Oh, you don't need that' or 'Why do you want

that?' You are all so supportive of each other." I think Southern women from girlhood learn respect and great love for each other, and we cling to this lifelong support system. Of course, when we get together, we're not always so nice about other people. We do gossip, but we always, always keep each other's secrets.

Sometimes men do come to our luncheons. They enjoy being in on the gossip and good food, even if they don't admit it. There is something quite decadent about a beautiful luncheon. These days, most men and women have to steal an hour or two away from work, heightening the fun and putting a little drama into everyday life. Once my friend Greg Parker gave a luncheon for Paul Newman and invited me as a guest, even though I was doing all the food. I was so thrilled, against my better judgment, I accepted. I usually refuse to be a guest at parties I cater—but Paul Newman! The minute I sat down, I looked at him and announced to the whole crowd, "I think my favorite movie of yours was *Picnic*." Without missing a beat, he said, "Susan, your food is wonderful, but your memory is not. I wasn't in *Picnic*; that was William Holden." That story

comes under most embarrassing moments in the catering business. Another time, I insensitively told Kenneth Branagh, who was in Savannah filming *The Gingerbread Man* in 1998, I'd have to take three Ritalin pills to watch his movie *Hamlet*. Sometimes my mouth just gets away from my head.

Some luncheons do have a higher purpose than gossip and respite from work. I cater a lot of parties at Helen Downing's because she generously opens her home often for charitable fundraisers. This handsome Italianate townhouse on Chippewa Square was designed for John Stoddard by the New York architect John Norris in 1867. Helen's is an easy place in which to entertain graciously because of its beautifully detailed interiors and her period furnishings. One luncheon Helen gave was for a group of out-of-town people. I'm sure three-fourths of them had never heard of tomato pie, and most of them were afraid of grits. Grits are a mainstay of a Southern diet. Growing up, we ate grits and noodles all the time because we were relatively poor (Daddy was with the railroad, and Mother was a nurse). We didn't realize that our family was so ahead of our time. Noodles are now pasta and you find grits on menus of many famous New York restaurants.

People love to guess what's in my shrimp and grits. They are always fascinated by the yellow color and ask what causes it. I really didn't know. So one day I asked my cook, Donna, "Do you put curry in that?"

"No."

"Turmeric?"

"No."

"Well, what makes it yellow?"

"Yellow food coloring. Just to give it a little better presentation, don't ya know!" ≶

Recipes

Emmie Winburn's Cucumber Soup

Serves 6

When the weather is hot, which is most of the summer months, I keep a bowl of this in the refrigerator and dip it up for a light lunch. So refreshing!

2 TABLESPOONS BUTTER

6 CUCUMBERS

1 LEEK, WHITE PART ONLY, SLICED

1 BAY LEAF

1 TABLESPOON ALL-PURPOSE FLOUR

3 CUPS CHICKEN STOCK*

SALT

1 CUP HEAVY CREAM

BLACK PEPPER

JUICE OF 1/2 LEMON

SOUR CREAM

1 TEASPOON FRESH DILL OR MINT, CHOPPED

Peel, seed, and chop 5 of the cucumbers. Melt the butter in a medium saucepan over low heat. Add the sliced cucumbers, leek, and bay leaf and sauté for 20 minutes. Remove the bay leaf. Stir in flour to make a paste. Add the stock and 1 teaspoon salt. Simmer for 30 minutes.

Transfer the soup to a food processor and process until smooth. Strain and discard the solids. Chill the soup for several hours until cold.

Stir the cream into the soup. Season with salt and pepper. Add the lemon juice. Chop the remaining cucumber. Serve with a dab of sour cream, a sprinkling of fresh dill, and the chopped cucumber. ⤳

Stock would be preferred here. A good-quality canned chicken broth can be substituted.

Shrimp Salad

Serves 4

Everyone makes shrimp salad, but mine is very simple. I leave the shrimp whole.

2 POUNDS MEDIUM SHRIMP, PEELED AND DEVEINED WITH TAILS REMOVED

1 STALK CELERY, FINELY DICED

3 HARD-COOKED EGGS, PEELED AND GRATED

1/4 TEASPOON WHITE PEPPER

1/2 CUP MAYONNAISE

To cook the shrimp, bring a pot of salted water to a boil. Drop the shrimp in and cook until they turn pink, 3 minutes. Drain well.

Combine the shrimp, celery, and eggs in a bowl. Add the pepper and mayonnaise to shrimp salad and toss. Refrigerate until you are ready to serve. ⤳

MY ANNUAL TRIP TO PROVENCE, FRANCE, WITH ITS MANY BEAUTIFUL FIELDS OF SUNFLOWERS, INSPIRED THIS PRESENTATION.

CATERING TIPS ❧ SUNFLOWER CAVIAR

24 EGGS

½ CUP MAYONNAISE

2 TABLESPOONS MR. MUSTARD OR OTHER SPICY MUSTARD

2 TABLESPOONS CHOPPED WHITE ONION

½ TEASPOON SALT

½ TEASPOON WHITE PEPPER

1½ CUPS SOUR CREAM

8 TO 10 OUNCES CAVIAR

12 ENDIVES, LEAVES CLEANED AND SEPARATED

In a saucepan, cover the eggs with cold water and bring to a boil. When the water comes to a full boil, cover tightly with a lid and turn the heat off. Let the eggs sit for 15 minutes. Peel the eggs and save the whites for another use. Mash the egg yolks with the mayonnaise and mustard until creamy. Add the onion, salt, and pepper. Mound in an oblong ball shape on a serving tray. Cover the entire ball with sour cream. In the meantime, if you are using grocery store caviar in a jar, put it in a strainer and run cold water over it until the water runs clear. Place caviar over the entire mound. Take endive leaves and stick them into the base of the mound.

Create layers of leaves around base for a sunflower petal effect. The leaves are then used to dip into and eat the center of the flower. ❧

Baby Greens Salad with Candied Walnuts and 45 South Dressing

Serves 6 to 8

Candied Walnuts
1 cup walnut halves
½ cup confectioners' sugar
Vegetable oil, for frying
¼ teaspoon salt
⅛ teaspoon cayenne pepper

45 South Dressing
1 cup balsamic vinegar
7 tablespoons Dijon mustard
7 tablespoons light brown sugar
1 cup olive oil
1 cup vegetable oil

2 Bosc pears cut in wedges
5 to 6 ounces of mesclun greens
½ cup dried cranberries
8 ounces fresh goat cheese, cut into 1-ounce circles

One of my favorite restaurants, 45 South, makes a delicious salad dressing. Every time I ask for the recipe, I get the runaround. My cooks and I made this one up and call it 45 South Dressing, just for spite! This is a great salad with which to start or end a meal. If I serve it after the meal, I serve it with fresh pear slices.

In a medium saucepan, cover the walnut halves with cold water. Bring to a boil. Reduce the heat, and simmer for 5 minutes or until slightly softened. Drain the walnuts and transfer to paper towels to dry. In a bowl, stir together the walnuts and confectioners' sugar.

In a heavy pot, heat 3 inches of vegetable oil to 350° F. Add the walnuts in batches and fry for 1 to 2 minutes until they are crisp. Transfer the walnuts as they are fried with a slotted spoon to a baking sheet. Season with salt and cayenne. Let cool.

To make dressing, blend vinegar, mustard, and brown sugar in a food processor. Slowly add the oils with the motor running. It will be thick.

Toss together greens, cranberries, and walnuts. Drizzle with dressing and top with pears. Store remaining dressing in refrigerator for up to 2 weeks. ⇒

Sylvia's Chicken Pot Pie

Serves 6

2½ to 3 pound chicken
1 (1-quart) can chicken broth
2 cups water

White sauce

4 cups chicken broth (reserved from cooking chicken)
Seasoning salt
½ cup all-purpose flour
1 cup half-and-half
8 ounces white mushrooms, whole
1 cup pearl onions
1 cup sliced carrots
5 to 6 tablespoons unsalted butter
1 cup frozen green peas, thawed

Crust

2 cups all-purpose flour, sifted
1 teaspoon salt
¾ cup vegetable shortening
1 egg, separated
5 tablespoons cold water

Sylvia Spann, my sister, also got the cooking gene from our mother. Sylvia raised three boys, and, I'm convinced, never opened a can. She probably used fresh peas in this recipe. She cooked three meals a day and all from scratch. This is one of my favorite meals and one of the few things I freeze!

Set the chicken in a large pot and cover with the broth and water. Bring to a boil and then simmer for 30 minutes. Let cool in the broth. Remove meat in chunks from bones. Strain broth and reserve. Save any remaining stock for another use. Bones and skin can be thrown away.

Season the broth with seasoning salt. Bring 4 cups of broth to a boil. Make a slurry by slowly adding ½ cup hot broth to the flour in a bowl. Whisk these together until smooth. Whisk into the remaining broth. Turn heat to medium. Stir constantly for several minutes until thick and smooth. Add the half-and-half and stir until smooth. Set aside.

Over medium heat, sauté mushrooms, onions, and carrots in butter in a skillet until onions are translucent. Drain in colander. Place in 9 by 13-inch casserole dish along with the chicken and peas. (Five individual 5 by 1½-inch round dishes can be used instead.) Cover with white sauce and set aside while making crust.

Preheat the oven to 425° F.

To make the crust, combine the flour and salt. Cut in the shortening until the mixture resembles coarse meal. In a small bowl, beat the egg yolk with the water and pour into flour mixture. Stir to make a soft dough.

On a lightly floured surface, roll out the dough to a thickness of ½ inch and place on top of the filling. Put a couple of slits on top. Brush with the egg white.

Bake for 20 to 25 minutes, until crust is brown. Serve hot. ⸙

Susan's Tomato Pie

Serves 6 to 8

I served this at an out-of-town wedding luncheon where the groom was from New York City. Twenty guests asked for the recipe, and I now envision tomato pies being served all over Manhattan.

9-INCH PIE SHELL, BAKED

2 TABLESPOONS DIJON MUSTARD

4 TOMATOES, PEELED AND SLICED

SALT AND FRESHLY GROUND BLACK PEPPER

4 OUNCES WHITE CHEDDAR CHEESE, GRATED

4 OUNCES CHEDDAR CHEESE, GRATED

½ CUP MAYONNAISE

⅓ CUP FRESHLY GRATED PARMESAN CHEESE

Preheat the oven to 350° F.

Spread the pie shell with Dijon mustard. Layer the sliced tomatoes, salt and pepper, and cheddar cheeses in the pie shell, ending with the cheese.

Mix together the mayonnaise and Parmesan cheese in a small bowl. Spread on top of the pie. Bake for about 20 minutes, until bubbly. Let cool. Serve at room temperature.

Shrimp and Tasso Gravy over Creamy White Grits

Serves 6 to 8

Grits

2 CUPS COARSE STONE-GROUND QUICK
WHITEGRITS (WASHED)
6 CUPS WATER
SALT
1 CUP CHICKEN BROTH
1 CUP HEAVY CREAM
¼ CUP (½ STICK) UNSALTED BUTTER
FRESHLY GROUND PEPPER

Tasso Gravy

¼ CUP (½ STICK) UNSALTED BUTTER
½ CUP SLICED TASSO, DICED (SMOKED HAM CAN
BE SUBSTITUTED)
½ CUP ALL-PURPOSE FLOUR
4 CUPS CHICKEN BROTH
1 TABLESPOON OLD BAY SEASONING
1 TEASPOON LAWRY'S SEASONED SALT
2 POUNDS SHRIMP, PEELED AND DEVEINED

One of my most successful dishes to serve at brunches, luncheons, and cocktail parties. Donna, one of my best cooks, adds a little yellow food coloring to make it more lively.

Wash the grits by putting them in a colander and running cold water over them. Bring the water and ½ teaspoon salt to a boil in a heavy-bottomed saucepan. Slowly pour in the grits, stirring constantly. When the grits start boiling, add the broth. Decrease the heat to low and stir constantly so the grits do not settle to the bottom. In about 5 minutes, the grits will plump up and become a thick mass. Continue to cook the grits for 20 to 25 minutes, stirring frequently. The grits should have absorbed all of the liquid and become soft.

Stir in the heavy cream and cook for another 10 minutes, until the grits are thick, like oatmeal. Add butter and cook until melted. Season with salt and pepper. Transfer to a plate and set aside.

To blanch the shrimp, bring a large pot of salted water to a boil. Drop the shrimp in and reduce to a simmer. Cook the shrimp in simmering water for 3 to 5 minutes, until pink. Drain well.

To make the gravy, melt the butter in a medium saucepan over low heat. Add the tasso. Sauté for 1 minute, until the meat is slightly browned. Make a roux by adding the flour and stirring until well combined. Add the chicken broth to the roux, stirring vigorously. Keep stirring constantly until the broth begins to thicken. Add Old Bay Seasoning and Lawry's Seasoned Salt. Drop the shrimp into the hot gravy. Heat a few more minutes. Then add the gravy on top of the grits and serve. ☞

Almond Rocha

Serves 20

My friend and former catering partner, Lois Ashcraft, gave me this recipe. It is all about the whisking!

1 CUP SLICED ALMONDS (WITH BROWN EDGES)
1 CUP (2 STICKS) SALTED BUTTER
1 CUP SUGAR
12 (1.45-OUNCE) HERSHEY'S MILK CHOCOLATE WITH ALMONDS BARS

Cover a 17 by 12-inch cookie sheet with aluminum foil. Sprinkle half the almonds on the sheet.

Put the butter and sugar in a heavy skillet and cook over high heat. Start whisking when melted. Whisk constantly until the mixture turns a deep caramel color (do not burn). This process takes about 20 to 25 minutes of constant whisking. Spread mixture over the almonds on the prepared cookie sheet.

Melt the Hershey's bars in top of double boiler over simmering water. Whisk until smooth. Spread the melted chocolate on top of the caramel mixture. Sprinkle the remaining $1/2$ cup almonds on top. Let cool and then cover with foil. Refrigerate until you are ready to serve, then break into 1-inch pieces.

Palm Beach Brownies

Serves 32

8 ounces (8 squares) unsweetened baking chocolate

1 cup (2 sticks) unsalted butter

5 large or extra-large eggs

3¾ cups sugar

2½ tablespoons dry instant espresso or other (powdered) instant coffee

1 tablespoon vanilla extract

1 teaspoon almond extract

¼ teaspoon salt

1⅔ cups sifted all-purpose flour

8 ounces (generous 2 cups) walnut halves or large pieces

Once you taste these you will know why they are called Palm Beach Brownies. They are so rich! I like to dust the top with powdered sugar.

Adjust the rack one-third up from bottom of the oven. Preheat the oven to 400° F.

Line a 9 by 13-inch baking pan with foil by first inverting the pan, covering it with a long piece of foil, then molding the foil to the shape of the pan. Turn the pan right side up and carefully press the foil into the pan without tearing it. Brush the foil with soft or melted butter, or use a nonstick spray.

Combine the chocolate and butter in the top of a double boiler set over hot water over medium heat (or in a small heavy saucepan over low heat). Stir occasionally until the chocolate and butter are melted. Stir to mix. Remove from the heat and set aside.

In the large bowl of an electric mixer, beat the eggs with the sugar, instant coffee, vanilla, almond extract, and salt at high speed for 10 minutes. Add the chocolate mixture and beat on low speed only until mixed. Then add the flour. Again, beat on low speed only until mixed. Stir in the nuts. Pour into the prepared pan and smooth the top.

Bake for 30 minutes. If the brownies seem to be turning quite dark at the edges, remove from the oven. Otherwise continue baking for another 5 minutes. There will be a thick crust on top and a toothpick inserted in the center will not come out clean.

Allow to cool in the pan on a rack to room temperature. Then invert the pan onto a rack, peel off the foil, invert again, and allow to stand for 6 to 8 hours, or overnight. Cut into bars or squares. Wrap the brownies individually. Do not allow them to dry out. ⚘

Lemon Squares

Makes 24 squares

Shortbread Crust

2 cups all-purpose flour
1 cup (2 sticks) unsalted butter, at
room temperature
½ cup confectioners' sugar
¼ teaspoon salt

Lemon Filling

4 large eggs
2 cups granulated sugar
⅓ cup fresh lemon juice
Zest grated from 1 lemon
1 teaspoon baking powder
1 teaspoon salt
¼ cup all-purpose flour

Confectioners' sugar for dusting

I make these in Pyrex dishes, for the ease.

Preheat the oven to 350° F. Prepare a 9 by 13-inch baking pan by coating with a nonstick spray.

To make the crust, mix the ingredients in a large bowl until smooth. Gather into a ball and place in the middle of baking pan. Then press into the bottom.

Bake for 15 to 20 minutes, until golden brown. Let the crust cool while the filling is being made. Reduce the oven temperature to 300° F.

To make the filling, whisk together the eggs and sugar until well blended. Stir in the lemon juice, lemon zest, baking powder, salt, and flour. Pour over the shortbread crust.

Bake for 20 to 25 minutes until the filling is set. Cool completely. Sprinkle with confectioners' sugar. Cut into 24 squares. ✒

Key Lime Pie

Serves 8

A heavenly dessert. Sometimes I offer my guest a choice of the pecan or key lime pie. Key lime pie always wins. I put whipping cream and a lime slice on top. I usually make my own graham cracker crust from the recipe on the graham cracker box.

1 (14-ounce) can sweetened condensed milk
½ cup fresh lime juice
1 teaspoon grated lime zest
2 egg yolks
1 (9-inch) graham cracker crust

Preheat the oven to 325° F.

Mix together the milk, lime juice, lime zest, and egg yolks. Beat until smooth. Pour the mixture into the crust.

Bake for 15 minutes. It should be firm to touch. Cool in the refrigerator for several hours before serving. ⮑

Picnics, Peaches, and Pearls

Savannah is temperate most of the year, so outdoor parties on high river bluffs, in beautiful gardens, and at the seashore are popular. If you are clever, you can get rid of most of the bugs before your guests arrive. In Savannah we say that if it weren't for the bugs, you'd think you were in heaven. The soft, cooling breezes that make Spanish moss sway and palm trees rustle are an integral part of our city's charm.

Most garden parties are in the spring, when all Savannah is in bloom. Azaleas peak from the middle to the end of March. Savannah's fabled St. Patrick's Day celebration (March 17) brings thousands of tourists, many of whom stay for the Tour of Homes and other festive spring events that take advantage of our beautiful flowers and weather that time of year. Garden parties are sought-after invitations because they give ladies an excuse to buy a new hat and wear their pearls. Many Southern girls have at least one strand that dates back to her grandmother. And men love to wear their seersucker suits, which belong at a garden party like tuxedos belong at a ball.

A mid-morning brunch, a luncheon, and a tea party in the afternoon are all excuses for a garden party. This is one time you don't have to use fine china; you can serve food in all kinds of colored pottery and decorate with a little whimsy.

My friend Lorraine's gorgeous side garden is an ideal place for a spring garden party. Landscaped by her brother-in-law, Ryan Gainey, the famous garden designer and author, the garden is laid out on the site of an old garage at the side of the house. When the garage was demolished, the walls were left intact to enfold the plantings and give this space the air of a secret garden, which so many downtown Savannah gardens are. The architecture of Savannah's old Federal townhouses only allows for small patio gardens at the rear of the house or side gardens off side porches in the Charleston tradition. These tight outdoor rooms provide an intimate setting for a kind of entertaining Savannahians enjoy.

Located on the water—actually shot through with tidal rivers—Savannah is a natural venue for boating parties. At one time I catered parties practically every week for a local bank on its 67-foot Trumpy yacht, *The Flying Lady*. My staff developed sea legs serving shrimp and crab on a rolling sea, and I developed a lot of casserole recipes. They were prepared in my commercial kitchen, then warmed up in the tiny galley aboard ship. I'm very fortunate that many

of my clients have boats as well as beautiful homes in which to showcase my food. One such friend is Dr. Albert Wall, who came to my rescue in quite an unusual and special circumstance.

Of all the movie stars for whom I've catered, Tom Hanks was my favorite. He was in town for several weeks filming *Forrest Gump*. I'd been doing food for the cast and crew and saw him around, but I'd never really met him. Then one day, out of the blue, his assistant called and asked me to do a special dinner for Tom's wife, Rita Wilson, on her birthday. Tom wanted to charter a yacht and take her on a cruise for a romantic birthday dinner. I called Albert, whose boat I knew would be perfect. On the evening of the event, Albert and one crewman, my cook, Donna Edwards, my waiter, Keith Howington, and I went on board early to get everything ready. I took my own china and silver (something I often do even for people not so famous), armloads of fresh flowers, and a lot of candles out to the Savannah Yacht Club, where the boat was docked.

When Tom and Rita arrived everything was ready. They relaxed and had drinks in the open stern at the candlelit table. Albert and his mate cruised down the Wilmington River, past Moon River (made famous in the song of that name by Savannah songwriter Johnny Mercer, but that's another story). I cooked up a five-course dinner in the galley with the help of Donna and Keith. A couple of years later Rita was quoted in *People* magazine saying the most romantic thing Tom ever did was charter a yacht and take her on a moonlight cruise for her birthday. I beamed when I read that.

I have to mention one other kind of picnic I fix that is similar to a boating party. Gulfstream Aerospace is headquartered in Savannah, and I get requests to cater meals and parties on private jets. I usually send out plenty of hors d'oeuvres like pickled shrimp (*Pickled Shrimp, page 95*), jumbo lump crabmeat with my special pink sauce (*Jumbo Lump Crabmeat with Pink Sauce, page 96*), and terrines of pâté with fresh baguettes. Because it is unlikely that there will

be a cook aboard, I send cold meals of arranged salads—something like lobster tails or beef tenderloin, grilled vegetables, and some sumptuous dessert like lemon tarts with fresh berries and whipped cream.

One of the most heartfelt thanks I've ever received was from Bill Cosby. When his plane needed some repairs, he came along to see Savannah. He called me with the most gracious compliments about the food I sent out to his plane. This is the sort of thing not everyone does, especially busy, famous people, so I always remember that sort of personal touch with special appreciation.

A picnic I will never forget occurred one cold February day. The Savannah College of Art and Design (SCAD) asked me to cater box lunches for two hundred people on Sapelo Island for the dedication of a wonderful historic church SCAD students had renovated. Now, the only way to Sapelo is by boat. Paula Wallace, the President of SCAD, made a special request for pimento cheese sandwiches. Because they would have dried out had we made them the day before, my staff stayed up all night getting them ready. I even had to make a 2:00 a.m. run to the grocery in my pajamas for more cheese. We got the vans loaded, and off they went at about 6:30 in the morning. I stayed behind in the shop and was horrified to find all the pimento cheese sandwiches in the back cooler about an hour after they left. They had forgotten the one thing Paula wanted.

I immediately began trying to figure out how to get across the water with all those pimento cheese sandwiches. I started by calling my hairdresser, because he lived down there by St. Simons. He called everybody he knew and finally got in touch with some man who said the boat with my staff had left, but he offered to take me on his boat. I jumped in my car and got there in pretty good time to find this little boat and this nice little man.

Since I had planned to go to lunch with some friends, I had on a beautiful suit, my best jewels, and a new orange pashmina. We got ourselves and the sandwiches in the

boat, and away we flew. Freezing cold salt water splashing everywhere, I held on for dear life with my feet on top of the sandwich boxes. I kept thinking, "This boat is going to sink, and nobody will ever know I was on it, and my daughter will never get these jewels she wants because they will be buried with me at sea." When I finally got there, of course the picnic was over. I was giving away pimento cheese sandwiches for days. I still don't know who that man was. Oh, the things you have to do!

Garden parties in the spring give way to beach and boat parties in the summer, but in fall and winter most Savannahians look forward to oyster roasts for informal entertainment. Sweet, succulent local oysters are the stars of Low Country roasts from Charleston to Brunswick. Bluffton, a little summer settlement established on the May River in 1824, is just across the Savannah River in South Carolina. The Bluffton Oyster Company gathers fresh oysters daily in season (October to March), and anyone can buy them off the dock by the sack. I use Bluffton oysters for all my oyster recipes. They are small and sweeter than any other oysters I have ever tasted. I also get wonderful fresh seafood from Matthews Seafood. They buy from local commercial fishermen who work the Atlantic and nearby shores. Trey Matthews (Louis III) runs the business founded by his grandfather in 1896. I never, never use any seafood that has been frozen, and certainly no pasteurized crabmeat. If I can't get it fresh, I don't serve it.

For those of you who haven't been to an oyster roast, it's a sight to see—whole families attend from great-grandmothers to newborn babies. People who have houses on the rivers host them. There is usually a lot of drinking, the wonderful smell of roaring fires, and a lot of good eating. When the fire is raging and ready, some of the men place a large piece of sheet metal or a grate on blocks over the fire and the oysters onto the metal and quickly cover them with wet burlap (usually the sacks they came in). When the oysters begin to split, they are ready to be shoveled onto high wooden tables, around which everyone stands, shucking and eating. The table is covered with old newspapers and has oyster knives and garden gloves scattered among bowls of hot lemon butter (always with fresh-squeezed lemon juice) and cocktail sauces.

The oysters are just the first course of a great meal. After the oysters are gone and the fires have died, everyone goes inside for dinner (which, like Thanksgiving dinner, happens mid afternoon). If the hosts don't want to "put on" the roast, I hire somebody to do the oysters and concentrate on the bar and the food. People always want me to serve the same things: Savannah red rice, fried chicken, and ham sweet potato biscuits *(Ham Sweet Potato Biscuits, page 79)*. These parties never get boring and few people turn down such an invitation to spend the afternoon on the water.

I find myself suggesting the same picnic desserts at most of these informal parties. My coconut pound cake *(Coconut Pound Cake, page 102)*, is a favorite because it is not only delicious, but also easy to transport. People also love my praline pecan bars *(Creole Pecan Praline Bars, page 154)*. When peaches are in season, we make peach cobbler, peaches and cream, peach ice cream, and anything else we can think of. The reputation of Georgia peaches—the girls and the fruit—is well deserved! ⅌

Recipes

Curried Zucchini Soup

Serves 8

This recipe was given to me by a New York actress, who was then starring in **Les Miserables** *on Broadway. Passing through Savannah, she fell in love with the city and immediately planned a Savannah wedding, which I catered. This is one of my favorite soups. When I prepare this for parties, I always think of the beautiful actress and dancer who could also cook!*

6 medium zucchini, sliced
1 large onion, sliced
5 carrots, sliced
4 cups chicken broth
2 teaspoons curry powder
1 clove garlic
1 to 1½ cups heavy cream
1 teaspoon salt
½ teaspoon freshly ground black pepper
½ teaspoon Morton Nature's Seasons Seasoning Blend

Combine the zucchini, onion, carrots, chicken broth, curry powder, and garlic in a large saucepan. Simmer for 30 minutes. Let cool slightly. Blend in a food processor until smooth. Add cream according to the thickness you desire. Add the salt, pepper, and seasoning blend. Chill. Serve cold. ❧

Tomato-Avocado Ribbon Salad

Serves 6

Avocado Layer

2 teaspoons unflavored gelatin (1 envelope)
½ cup water
1 teaspoon salt
3 tablespoons fresh lemon juice
5 drops Tabasco sauce
1½ cups sieved avocado (4 to 5 small avocados pressed through fine mesh sieve or mashed up)
Few drops green food coloring

Cheese Layer

2 teaspoons unflavored gelatin (1 envelope)
½ cup cold water
4 (3-ounce) packages cream cheese, softened
½ cup milk
⅔ cup mayonnaise
2 tablespoons chopped green onion (scallion) tops
1 teaspoon salt
½ teaspoon Worcestershire sauce

Tomato Layer

3⅔ cups tomato juice
1 stalk celery, chopped
1 small onion, sliced
2 lemon slices
1 small bay leaf
1 teaspoon salt
⅛ teaspoon freshly ground black pepper
4 teaspoons unflavored gelatin (2 envelopes)
¼ cup apple cider vinegar

Lettuce, for garnish

This is a beautiful salad and very impressive to serve. The recipe is easy to put together but does take quite a bit of time. Ladies love it.

To make the avocado layer, sprinkle the gelatin over ¼ cup cold water in a small saucepan. Add ¼ cup boiling water. Add the salt, lemon juice, and Tabasco sauce. Cook over medium heat until thickened. Add the avocados and food coloring. Pour into a 9 by 5-inch loaf pan and chill until almost firm, several hours.

Start making the cheese layer when the avocado layer is almost firm. Sprinkle the gelatin over the cold water in the top of a double boiler and let soften for 5 minutes. Place the top of the double boiler over boiling water and heat until dissolved.

Beat together the cream cheese and milk in a large bowl. Stir in the mayonnaise, green onions, salt, and Worcestershire sauce. Stir in the gelatin. Pour over the avocado layer and chill until almost firm.

While the other layers are chilling, make the tomato layer. Combine 3 cups of the tomato juice, celery, onion, lemon, bay leaf, salt, and pepper in a medium saucepan. Simmer, uncovered, for 10 minutes. Strain and discard the solids. Sprinkle the gelatin over the remaining ⅔ cup tomato juice and vinegar in a large bowl. Let soften for 5 minutes. Stir in the hot mixture and continue stirring until the gelatin is dissolved. Pour the tomato mixture over the cream cheese layer and chill until set.

To serve, unmold onto a platter. Cut into 1½-inch slices and serve on a bed of lettuce. ⇝

Seafood and Artichoke Casserole

Serves 6 to 8

For 5 years I was the caterer on a 67-foot Trumpy yacht that was owned by a local bank. I lost the contract when the bank was bought by a larger bank, and the boat was given away. This was the most requested dish out of the many I offered. It can be put together ahead and heated up while guests are having drinks.

1 (14-OUNCE) CAN ARTICHOKES, DRAINED

1 POUND MEDIUM SHRIMP, PEELED AND DEVEINED, WITH TAILS REMOVED

1 POUND WHITE BACKFIN CRABMEAT, PICKED OVER FOR SHELL BITS

4½ TABLESPOONS BUTTER

4½ TABLESPOONS ALL-PURPOSE FLOUR

1½ CUPS HALF-AND-HALF

1 TABLESPOON WORCESTERSHIRE SAUCE

¼ CUP DRY SHERRY

JUICE OF ½ LEMON

SALT AND WHITE PEPPER

⅛ TEASPOON CAYENNE PEPPER

¼ CUP FRESHLY GRATED PARMESAN CHEESE

1 TEASPOON PAPRIKA

FRESHLY COOKED RICE, TO SERVE

Preheat the oven to 375° F. Butter a 3-quart baking dish.

To cook the shrimp, bring a pot of water to boil. Drop shrimp in and cook until they turn pink, about 3 minutes. Drain well.

Arrange the artichokes in the baking dish. Spread the shrimp and crabmeat over the artichokes.

In a large heavy saucepan, melt the butter over medium heat. Whisk in the flour to make a smooth paste. Cook and stir for 5 minutes. Slowly add the half-and-half, cooking and stirring constantly until thickened and smooth. Stir in Worcestershire sauce, sherry, lemon juice, salt, white pepper, and cayenne pepper. Pour over the ingredients in the baking dish. Sprinkle with cheese and paprika.

Bake for 20 minutes. Serve hot with rice. ⇝

Asparagus Quiche

Serves 8

Crust

1½ cups instant flour such as wondra
½ cup unsalted butter, cut into pieces
3 tablespoons vegetable shortening
⅓ cup ice water
½ teaspoon salt

Filling

3 large eggs
1¼ cups heavy cream
¼ cup chopped fresh parsley leaves
Salt
Freshly ground white pepper
7 to 8 stalks asparagus, bottoms trimmed
3 tablespoons butter
Freshly ground black pepper
½ cup grated gruyère cheese

I love this dish for any event, because if looks very pretty on a table. I have to confess, I often use a store-bought pie crust.

To make the crust, put the flour in a large bowl. Using two knives or a pastry cutter, cut the butter and vegetable shortening into the mixture until it resembles coarse meal. Add the ice water and salt and mix until the dough comes together. Form the dough into a ball. Wrap in waxed paper and refrigerate for 2 hours. Roll out the pastry on a floured surface to about ¼ inch thick. Fit it into a 9-inch quiche pan. Take a fork and press around edges to finish. Refrigerate for 1 hour.

Preheat the oven to 425° F.

Prick the bottom of the pie shell liberally with a fork. Place another smaller pan inside to help set the sides while baking, or place a sheet of foil in the shell and fill with beans, rice, or pie weights.

Bake for 5 to 7 minutes, until the pie shell begins to feel firm. Remove the inside pan (or weights), return the pie shell to the oven, and bake for 2 minutes. Use a fork to prick the pie shell, which will be lightly browned and puffed up. Remove from the oven and set aside on a wire rack to cool slightly. Don't turn off the oven.

Meanwhile, to make the filling, mix together the eggs, cream, parsley, ½ teaspoon salt, and white pepper in a medium-size bowl. Chill for at least 30 minutes. (Or cover tightly, and refrigerate for up to 1 day.) Pour one-third of the egg mixture into the partially baked quiche crust. Bake until the filling begins to set, about 10 minutes.

Meanwhile, cut the asparagus stalks in half. Melt 2 tablespoons of the butter in a medium-size skillet over medium heat. Add the asparagus and cook until tender, 4 to 6 minutes. The tips will cook faster than the bottoms, so remove them first. Season with the salt and black pepper and arrange in the quiche pan in a pretty pattern, like the spokes of a wheel. Pour the rest of the egg mixture over the asparagus. Sprinkle with the Gruyère cheese and dot with the remaining 1 tablespoon butter.

Bake for about 30 minutes, until puffed and brown. Serve hot or at room temperature.

Yellow Squash and Mozzarella Quiche with Fresh Thyme

Serves 6 to 8

Shell

1¼ cups unbleached all-purpose flour

½ teaspoon salt

½ cup (1 stick) unsalted butter, cut into ½-inch cubes

¼ cup (or more) ice water

Filling

1 tablespoon butter

12 ounces yellow crookneck squash (or other yellow summer squash), cut into ¼-inch rounds

2 teaspoons chopped fresh thyme

6 large eggs

1 cup whipping cream

¾ teaspoon salt

¼ teaspoon freshly ground black pepper

¼ teaspoon hot pepper sauce

¾ cup (packed) coarsely grated mozzarella cheese (about 3 ounces)

An unusual quiche, but delicious. The Mozzarella cheese makes the quiche very fluffy. I served this at my birthday luncheon and got rave reviews.

To make the shell, combine the flour and salt in a food processor and mix briefly. Add the butter and process until the mixture resembles coarse meal. Add the water and pulse until the dough comes together in moist clumps, adding more ice water by teaspoonfuls if the dough is dry. Gather the dough into a ball; flatten into a disk. Wrap and chill for at least 1 hour, up to 1 day.

Preheat the oven to 375° F.

Roll out the dough on a lightly floured surface to a 14½-inch round. Transfer to a 10-inch tart pan with a removable bottom. Fold under the overhang; press to form double-thick sides. Push the sides up until they are ¼ inch higher than top edge of pan. Pierce the crust all over with fork. Freeze for 10 minutes.

Line the dough with foil and dried beans or pie weights. Bake for about 25 minutes, until the sides are set. Remove the foil and beans. Return to the oven and bake for about 15 minutes more, until the shell is golden, piercing with a fork if the crust bubbles. Transfer the shell to a rack; cool completely.

Lower the oven temperature to 350° F.

To make the filling, melt the butter in heavy medium skillet over medium heat. Add the squash and thyme and sauté until the squash is just tender and translucent, about 5 minutes. Cool to room temperature.

Whisk the eggs, cream, salt, pepper, and hot sauce in a bowl. Arrange the squash over bottom of the crust. Sprinkle with the mozzarella. Pour the egg mixture into the crust, filling it completely. (Some egg mixture may be left over.) Place the tart pan on the middle oven rack.

Bake the quiche for about 35 minutes, until the filling is golden and set in center. Transfer the quiche to a wire rack and let cool for 15 minutes before serving. ❧

Lime Basil Chicken

Serves 8

This is a great dish to take on a picnic or serve at a ladies' luncheon. Be sure and garnish with fresh basil, because the aroma of the basil adds greatly to the success of this recipe.

4 POUNDS CHICKEN TENDERS (24 STRIPS)
6 CUPS CHICKEN BROTH OR STOCK
1 CUP MAYONNAISE
FRESH BASIL, TO GARNISH

Marinade
1 CUP FRESH LIME JUICE (ABOUT 8 LIMES)
4 CLOVES GARLIC, LIGHTLY CRUSHED
1/4 CUP TIGHTLY PACKED FRESH BASIL LEAVES
2 1/4 TEASPOONS CHOPPED FRESH TARRAGON
3 LARGE SHALLOTS, MINCED
1 CUP EXTRA VIRGIN OLIVE OIL
6 TABLESPOONS VEGETABLE OIL
1/4 TEASPOON SUGAR
SALT AND FRESHLY GROUND BLACK PEPPER

Combine the chicken strips with the broth in a medium saucepan over medium heat. Cook for 8 to 10 minutes with the broth just below a simmer, until the chicken is no longer pink inside. Let the chicken cool in the broth for at least 1 hour.

While the chicken is cooling, combine the marinade ingredients in a large bowl.

Drain the cooled chicken and place in the marinade. (The broth can be saved for another use.) Cover and refrigerate for 24 hours.

To serve, drain the chicken, reserving the marinade. Arrange on a platter.

Mix the mayonnaise with 1/2 cup of the reserved marinade. Drizzle on top of the chicken. Garnish with fresh basil leaves. ⚘

Pork Tenderloin with Mustard Sauce

Serves 6 to 8

2 TABLESPOONS HONEY
2 TABLESPOONS DIJON MUSTARD
2 TABLESPOONS EXTRA VIRGIN OLIVE OIL
2 (4-INCH) SPRIGS FRESH ROSEMARY, STEMS REMOVED,
AND NEEDLES CRUSHED SLIGHTLY TO RELEASE FLAVOR
1 TABLESPOON CRUSHED BLACK PEPPER
1 TABLESPOON YELLOW MUSTARD SEEDS (OPTIONAL)
1 TEASPOON SALT
2 PORK TENDERLOINS (2½ TO 3½ POUNDS TOTAL WEIGHT)

Mustard Sauce

¼ CUP DIJON MUSTARD
1 TABLESPOON POWDERED MUSTARD
2 TABLESPOONS APPLE CIDER VINEGAR
2 TABLESPOONS SUGAR
½ TEASPOON SALT
4 EGG YOLKS, BEATEN
1 CUP HEAVY CREAM

I always grill pork tenderloins because grilled tenderloins have better flavor than broiled ones. They are so pretty on a tray surrounded by fresh rosemary.

Combine the honey, mustard, oil, rosemary, pepper, mustard seeds, and salt in a shallow dish large enough to hold the tenderloins. Add the tenderloins, turn to coat, and marinate in refrigerator for at least 1 hour.

Meanwhile, make the sauce. Combine the two mustards, vinegar, sugar, salt, and beaten egg yolks in the top of a double boiler. Cook over simmering water, stirring constantly, until thickened, approximately 10 minutes. Cool slightly. Stir in the cream. Set aside at room temperature.

Prepare a fire in a grill or preheat the broiler. Grill or broil the pork until golden brown on all sides, firm to the touch, and an instant-read thermometer inserted into one of the tenderloins registers 140° F (12 to 15 minutes total cooking time).

Let the tenderloins rest on a cutting board for a few minutes. Slice the meat on the diagonal into thin slices and serve, passing the sauce on the side. ⪼

53

Heywood's Jalapeño Cornbread

Serves 6

My brother, Heywood, is probably the best cook in my family. He is constantly coming up with recipes which he faxes me with a note that always begins, "Susan, this is great!" This one really is great!

3 LARGE EGGS

1 CUP SOUR CREAM

1 (15-OUNCE) CAN CREAM-STYLE CORN

1½ CUPS CHOPPED GREEN ONIONS (SCALLIONS), GREEN AND WHITE PARTS

1 TABLESPOON CHOPPED FRESH JALAPEÑO PEPPER

½ TEASPOON BAKING SODA

½ TEASPOON SALT

½ TEASPOON SUGAR

6 OUNCES SHARP CHEDDAR CHEESE, GRATED

6 OUNCES MONTEREY JACK CHEESE, GRATED

1¼ CUPS YELLOW CORNMEAL

¼ CUP VEGETABLE OIL

Preheat the oven to 350° F.

Beat the eggs until well mixed in a large bowl. Mix in the sour cream, corn, green onions, jalapeño, baking soda, salt, and sugar. Stir until well blended. Stir in two-thirds of the cheddar cheese and two-thirds of the Monterey Jack cheese and mix well. Add the cornmeal and mix well.

Pour the oil into a 12-inch cast-iron skillet and heat over medium-high heat until the oil is smoking hot, swirling the oil as it heats to coat the bottom and sides of the skillet.

Pour the hot oil into the batter and stir around fast to melt the cheese. Pour the batter into the hot skillet. (This mixture can also be placed into 9 by 13-inch baking pan at this point.) Sprinkle the remaining cheddar and Monterey Jack cheese evenly on top.

Bake for 40 minutes, or until lightly browned and crispy on top. Let sit for 15 minutes before slicing and serving directly out of the skillet. ❧

Savannah Red Rice

Serves 8

¼ POUND BACON

2 POUNDS SMOKED BEEF OR PORK SAUSAGE, CUT UP INTO 1-INCH PIECES (I USE HILLSHIRE FARM'S BEEF)

½ CUP CHOPPED ONION

½ CUP CHOPPED CELERY

¼ CUP CHOPPED GREEN BELL PEPPER

2 CUPS CONVERTED RICE (I USE UNCLE BEN'S)

2 (14.5-OUNCE) CANS TOMATO SAUCE (I USE HUNT'S)

1 TABLESPOON SALT

¼ TEASPOON FRESHLY GROUND BLACK PEPPER

1 TEASPOON SUGAR

⅛ TEASPOON TABASCO SAUCE

An oyster roast favorite and one of my most requested recipes. A real Southern dish. Men love it.

Preheat oven to 350° F.

Fry the bacon in a large frying pan over high heat until crisp. Remove from the pan, crumble, and reserve.

Add the sausage, onion, celery, and green pepper to the bacon grease remaining in the pan and sauté over medium heat until the vegetables are soft. Add the rice, tomato sauce, crumbled bacon, salt, pepper, sugar, and Tabasco sauce. Cook, uncovered, on top of the stove over medium heat for 10 minutes.

Pour the rice mixture into a 9 by 13-inch greased casserole dish, cover tightly with foil, and cook until the rice has absorbed most of the liquid, about 1 hour. Serve hot. ≽

Peach Cobbler with Blueberries

Serves 8

Filling

3 pints blueberries, rinsed and stemmed

2 teaspoons grated lemon zest

2½ pounds peaches, peeled, pitted and sliced
in ¼-inch wedges

¼ cup light brown sugar

Pastry

¾ cup (1½ sticks) unsalted butter, cold

1½ cups all-purpose flour

¾ cup white sugar

2 teaspoons baking powder

¼ teaspoon salt

½ cup buttermilk

1 large egg, lightly beaten

Vanilla ice cream, to serve

This is a very easy cobbler. I am always asked for the recipe when I serve it, especially in the summer when the peaches are best.

Preheat the oven to 400° F.

To make the filling, combine the blueberries with the lemon zest in a medium bowl and set aside. In a second bowl, sprinkle the peach slices with the brown sugar and set aside.

To make the pastry, slice the butter into ¼-inch pats and place in a large bowl. Add the flour, sugar, baking powder, and salt. Using your hands or a pastry knife, combine the ingredients until the mixture resembles coarse cornmeal. Make a well in the middle of the flour and butter mixture and add the buttermilk and the egg. Stir to combine.

Spread a layer of half of the blueberries in a 9 by 13-inch baking pan. Cover with the peaches, then top with the remaining berries. Using a rubber spatula, dab the cobbler dough on top, smoothing it as much as possible.

Bake for 40 minutes, until the fruit is bubbling and crust is golden. Serve hot or at room temperature with vanilla ice cream. ⤳

Cream Cheese Pie

Serves 6 to 8

My college friend Linda James served this at a house party of sorority sisters from Auburn and we loved it. It brings back memories of old friendships, late nights, and lots of diet talk. Exclude this from your menu if everyone is trying to lose weight.

2 (8-OUNCE) PACKAGES CREAM CHEESE, SOFTENED

3 LARGE EGGS

1 CUP WHITE SUGAR

1 TEASPOON ALMOND EXTRACT

Topping

1 PINT (16 OUNCES) SOUR CREAM

⅔ CUP WHITE SUGAR

1 TEASPOON VANILLA EXTRACT

1 PINT STRAWBERRIES, HULLED AND SLICED

1 CUP WHIPPING CREAM

1 TABLESPOON CONFECTIONERS' SUGAR

Preheat the oven to 325° F.

Mix the cream cheese, eggs, sugar, and almond extract in a food processor and process until smooth. Pour into a 10-inch pie pan.

Bake for 45 minutes. Let stand for 20 minutes. It will fall, creating its own crust.

To make the topping, beat together the sour cream, sugar, and vanilla until well mixed. Pour on top of the cream cheese layer.

Bake for 20 to 30 minutes, until firm. Let cool, then refrigerate overnight. The pie will keep for 2 weeks in refrigerator. To serve, beat the whipping cream with the confectioners' sugar until stiff peaks form. Cut the pie into wedges and top each slice with a spoonful of strawberries and a dollop of whipped cream. ≷

Red Velvet Cake

Serves 12

Cake

1 cup buttermilk
1 teaspoon white vinegar
1 teaspoon baking soda
2½ cups self-rising flour
1 teaspoon unsweetened cocoa powder
½ teaspoon salt
1½ cups vegetable oil
1½ cups sugar
2 large eggs
2 tablespoons red food coloring
1 teaspoon pure vanilla extract

Cream Cheese Frosting

1 (8-ounce) package cream cheese, softened
½ cup (1 stick) unsalted butter,
at room temperature
1 (16-ounce) box confectioners' sugar
1 teaspoon vanilla extract
1 cup pecan pieces, chopped
Pecan halves, for decoration (optional)

Note: The frosting can be made one day ahead of time. Cover with plastic wrap and store in the refrigerator. Bring to room temperature before frosting the cake. You can substitute walnuts for the pecans.

This cake says special occasion like no other dessert. Donna, my fabulous cook, takes orders for this especially at holiday time, and I can hardly keep enough red food coloring in the shop.

Preheat the oven to 300° F. Grease and flour two 9-inch cake pans. Tap out any excess flour.

Combine the buttermilk, vinegar, and baking soda in a medium mixing bowl. Into a second mixing bowl, sift together the flour, cocoa, and salt.

In a large mixing bowl, combine the oil, sugar, and eggs. Beat with an electric mixer on high speed for 3 to 4 minutes, until thickened.

Alternately add the flour mixture and buttermilk mixture to the egg mixture, beating for at least 2 to 3 minutes after each addition. When all the ingredients have been added to the bowl, beat for another 3 to 4 minutes on high speed. Mix in the red food coloring and vanilla until smooth. Divide the batter equally between the two cake pans.

Bake on center rack in the oven for about 45 minutes, until a tester inserted in the center of the cake comes out clean.

Cool 10 minutes in the pan. Turn out onto a wire rack and let cool completely before frosting.

To make the frosting, combine the cream cheese, butter, confectioners' sugar, and vanilla in a medium-size mixing bowl. Mix with an electric mixer on high speed for 3 to 4 minutes, until completely combined and smooth. Add the pecan pieces and mix until just combined.

Frost the first cake round on top about ½ inch thick with frosting, avoiding the edges by about ½ inch. Put the second cake round on top and press slightly to line up with the first round. Frost the sides, then the top. Decorate with pecan halves, if desired. ⇥

Cocktails, Couture, and Crudités

My favorite party to cater is a cocktail party because I can show off my food so easily on other people's beautiful silver and china. Cocktail parties are a Savannah tradition, and they are given more often than any other kind of party. Savannah men like their bourbon straight, and it's usually Jack Daniels. I know a Savannah couple whose dogs are named Jack and Soda. A cocktail party in Savannah is a dressy event. Men love their coats and ties, and women, of course, love a chance to show off their jewelry. The little black dress was invented for cocktail parties and won't ever go out of style here. I have one friend who has a whole closet full of nothing but cocktail dresses.

Cora Bett Thomas is one of my favorite clients; she always comes in after the party has started, looking marvelous and relaxed. A successful business woman, she entertains clients and associates in her home fairly often. Cora Bett has great confidence in me and my staff and knows that I'll have flowers on the tables, candles lit, and music playing. I do simple arrangements using one type of flower, such as a dozen or so roses cut short in a glass cube. I run hot water over the tops of the buds to separate the petals, open them up a bit, and put them in hot water. A single flower in a striking vase can be dramatic and economical. I often decorate my trays with flowers, such as sprays of cymbidium orchids. I also use square trays with a thin layer of something like black beans, which I spray with a nonstick spray, then top with Parmesan cheese rounds. You can also use other kinds of beans or uncooked rice for a nice presentation for passed hors d'oeuvre platters.

I decorate cheese trays by scattering tons of raspberries over the whole platter or tucking Champagne grapes in between the cheeses. I almost never do a party without my famous tomato sandwiches. On platters I put rows of the little round sandwiches with a snippet of parsley in the

middle of each one to decorate it, and then I scatter little grape tomatoes over the platter. People also love my cabbages. I find one really good head of cabbage, and then I start pulling a leaf from maybe thirty others. They never know how to charge me when I check out. We pin all those extra leaves to the whole cabbage and spray the whole thing with a nonstick spray and polish it, and it looks gorgeous. Then I put the cabbage masterpiece on a meat tray or something like that.

I buy most of my fresh produce from a local farm stand called Polk's, which for years was out near Sandfly, where Justice Clarence Thomas grew up. They keep a huge vat of freshly boiled peanuts, and the whole time I am shopping and chatting with folks, I am eating those peanuts. Every single time I get back to the shop with paper bags of tomatoes, okra, field peas, or whatever, I find a bag of those boiled peanuts tucked in somewhere as a surprise. I think Mr. Polk must know that peanuts have a special place in my heart because my hometown of Dothan is called "The Peanut Capital of the World." Boiled peanuts are a favorite all over South Georgia,

where peanuts are grown. Jimmy Carter still has his peanut farm in Plains. To make them, boil raw peanuts (in their shells) for an hour or so in salty water. They are great hot or cold.

I actually was hired to cater the wedding reception of an old boyfriend in the Cincinnati House. One of the most interesting houses in Savannah, it was left to the Society of Cincinnati by Alida Harper Fowles, whose brother was a member because, like all members, he was a descendent of someone who fought with George Washington in the Revolutionary War. Mrs. Fowles left the house intact with all her beautiful antiques, original chandeliers, and mantel pieces. Designed by the architect Charles Cluskey for Champion McAlpin, the house has been carefully maintained, and, recently, splendid gardens have been added. Just to show the groom what he had passed up, I used my most elegant decorating ideas and my best recipes, including my crab cakes, the most popular thing I do. I feel like I could have a party and only serve crab cakes and tomato sandwiches and everybody would be happy. The reason my crab cakes are so good is that they have no filler—they are simply the best jumbo lump crabmeat with mayonnaise, eggs, and some seasonings. I have one person who makes them, and for years people have been asking Annette Jackson for her recipe. She just responds, "I can't tell you that. You want me to lose my job?" So Annette, with your permission, I am giving out your crab cake recipe! ⤳

Recipes

Crab Mousse

Serves 10 to 12

I like to mold this mousse in a shell-shaped pan and unmold it onto a cake stand. It is very pretty for a party if you put whole cooked crab around the mold. Additional garnish such as sliced cucumbers, tomatoes, and lettuce or watercress will add even more to the presentation. This is an adaptation of a lobster mousse. It is just as tasty and a lot less expensive.

$1\frac{1}{2}$ TABLESPOONS UNFLAVORED GELATIN

$\frac{1}{4}$ CUP COLD WATER

$\frac{3}{4}$ CUP MAYONNAISE

3 TABLESPOONS FRESH LEMON JUICE

$\frac{1}{4}$ SMALL ONION, GRATED

2 POUNDS JUMBO LUMP CRABMEAT

$\frac{1}{3}$ CUP HEAVY CREAM

SALT AND FRESHLY GROUND BLACK PEPPER

Sprinkle the gelatin over the cold water in the top of a double boiler. Let soften for 5 minutes. Place the top of the double boiler over simmering water and stir until the gelatin is dissolved. Remove from the heat. Stir in the mayonnaise. Add the lemon juice. Fold the onion and crabmeat into the mayonnaise mixture.

Whip the cream in a large bowl until stiff peaks form. Fold the crab mixture into the whipped cream and season with salt and pepper. Turn the mixture into a 1-quart loaf pan or mold that has been prepared with a nonstick spray. Chill overnight or until firm. When you are ready to serve, turn out the mousse using a knife to loosen the edges. ⁊

Coconut Shrimp

Serves 8 to 10

This is a very popular passed hors d'oeuvres. It should be served hot. I leave the shrimp tails on so they are easily picked up by the guests. Serve with the orange marmalade sauce. Be sure and have two waiters serve these as one should offer the discard dish for the shrimp tails. I also use this recipe for coconut chicken. Just substitute chicken strips for the shrimp.

1½ POUNDS LARGE RAW SHRIMP (TAIL ON), PEELED AND DEVEINED

2 CUPS UNSWEETENED SHREDDED COCONUT

½ CUP ALL-PURPOSE FLOUR

½ CUP CORNSTARCH

1 TABLESPOON SALT

½ TEASPOON WHITE PEPPER

2 TABLESPOONS VEGETABLE OIL, PLUS ADDITIONAL OIL FOR FRYING

1 CUP ICE WATER

Sauce

½ CUP ORANGE MARMALADE

¼ CUP DIJON MUSTARD

¼ CUP HONEY

3 TO 4 DROPS TABASCO SAUCE

Wash the shrimp and dry well on paper towels. Set aside. Put the coconut in a food processor and pulse to chop finely.

To make the batter, in a medium bowl, combine the flour, cornstarch, salt, and white pepper. Mix well. Add 2 tablespoons oil and the ice water. Stir to blend.

To make the sauce, combine marmalade, mustard, honey, and Tabasco in a small bowl and mix well. Set aside.

Heat 4 cups of vegetable oil to 350° F in a deep fryer or a 12-inch skillet. Spread about ½ cup of the coconut on a flat pan. Dip the shrimp in batter, then roll in coconut, and fry in the hot oil until lightly browned, about 4 minutes. If you are using a skillet, turn the shrimp after 2 minutes. Drain cooked shrimp on paper towels. Continue dipping and frying shrimp, adding more coconut to the pan as needed. Serve the shrimp immediately, passing the sauce on the side. ⤳

Fried Oysters with Tarragon Tartar

Serves 10 to 12

I serve these oysters in silver teaspoons. I put a dollop of tartar sauce in each spoon and lay an oyster on top. I place a silver bowl in the center of the tray for the discarded spoons and pass around the tray for rave reviews.

Tartar Sauce

1 CUP MAYONNAISE

3 SHALLOTS, CHOPPED

1 TABLESPOON TARRAGON VINEGAR

2 TABLESPOONS CHOPPED FRESH TARRAGON

2 TABLESPOONS CAPERS

Oysters

1 PINT (APPROXIMATELY 50) SHUCKED BLUFFTON OR OTHER FRESH OYSTERS

1 TO 1½ CUPS ALL-PURPOSE COATING (I USE GOLDEN DIP ALL PURPOSE BREADING MIX)

VEGETABLE OIL, FOR FRYING

Mix all the ingredients for the tartar sauce in a bowl; set aside.

Heat 4 cups of oil in a 12-inch skillet over medium-high heat. Throw in a drop of water. When it sizzles, the oil is ready.

Pick through the oysters to remove any shells. Pour the coating mixture into a shallow bowl. Dredge the oysters in the coating. Fry on medium-high, turning once, until they curl and are golden brown, about 5 minutes total. Drain on paper towels. Serve while hot.

Serve each oyster on top of a dollop of tartar sauce in a silver teaspoon. ⤳

Seared Tuna with Wasabi Crème Fraîche

Serves 8

Only prepare this when you can get sushi-grade tuna because you are serving this tuna rare. I put it on skewers for cocktail parties.

Wasabi Crème Fraîche
1 CUP HEAVY WHIPPING CREAM
1 CUP SOUR CREAM
1 TO 2 (4.2-OUNCE) TUBES WASABI PASTE

4 POUNDS SUSHI-GRADE TUNA
CRACKED BLACK PEPPER
SESAME SEEDS
KOSHER SALT TO TASTE
3 TABLESPOONS EXTRA VIRGIN OLIVE OIL

Mix the cream and sour cream in a bowl and leave out at room temperature for approximately 6 hours. Then add 1 tube of the wasabi paste and mix well. Add additional wasabi if you'd like it hotter. Cover tightly and store in the refrigerator until you are ready to serve.

Sprinkle the tuna with cracked black pepper, sesame seeds, and kosher salt.

Heat the oil in a large heavy skillet over high heat. When the skillet is very hot, add the tuna and sear, 1 to 2 minutes on each side. Cool, cut into 1-inch thick slices, and thread onto skewers. Serve with a bowl of the wasabi crème fraîche in the middle. ⇗

Crab Cakes

Makes 10

My signature dish. If I could figure out how to mass-produce these, I'd be rich!

½ cup mayonnaise (I use Hellmann's)
1 red bell pepper, finely chopped
2 green onions (scallions), white and tender green parts, finely chopped
2 tablespoons Dijon mustard
2 teaspoons Old Bay Seasoning
⅛ teaspoon cayenne pepper
1 dash Worcestershire sauce
2 large egg yolks
2 pounds jumbo lump crabmeat
6 cups fresh bread crumbs
Vegetable oil, for frying

Mix together the mayonnaise, bell pepper, green onion, mustard, Old Bay Seasoning, cayenne, Worcestershire sauce, and egg yolks. Gently stir in the crabmeat. Put bread crumbs on a cookie sheet. Mold the crab cake with one hand and pat the cake with bread crumbs using the other hand. Form into 10 crab cakes, 3 inches wide and ½ inch thick. Each cake will need ¾ cup of bread crumbs.

Heat 4 cups of oil in a 12-inch skillet over medium-high heat. Add a single layer of crab cakes and fry in the oil, turning three or four times until crispy on outside, about 5 minutes on each side. Drain on paper towels. Serve hot. ❧

Parmesan Cheese Rounds

Makes 48 rounds

1 cup mayonnaise (I use hellmann's)
½ cup freshly grated Parmesan cheese
1 loaf thin sandwich bread
10 to 12 small white onions (pearl or boiling onions), very thinly sliced
Yellow mustard

Bar none, this is my most requested passed hors d'oeuvre. Delicious and inexpensive to make.

Preheat the broiler to 425° F.

Using a whisk, mix together the mayonnaise and Parmesan cheese in a small bowl.

With a 2⅛-inch cookie cutter, cut 2 rounds out of each slice of bread. Arrange the rounds on a baking sheet and place 5 inches from the heat source. Toast the bread on one side until they are golden brown, about 3 to 5 minutes.

Remove the bread from the oven and turn the rounds over to the untoasted sides. Spread each with a thin layer of mustard. Put 1 onion slice on top and cover with about 1 teaspoon of the mayonnaise mixture, spreading the mixture across the onion and bread.

Broil for about 1 minute until golden. Never take your eyes off these; the time varies with different ovens. Work in batches of 24 rounds. Serve one batch hot while the next is cooking. ❧

THIS MAKES A STRIKING ADDITION TO ANY CRUDITÉ TABLE. ALTHOUGH, UNLIKE THE EDIBLE STRAWBERRY TREE (SEE PAGE 117), THE ASPARAGUS TREE IS STRICTLY A CENTERPIECE.

CATERING TIPS ～ ASPARAGUS TREE

PLASTER OF PARIS
8 IN. WIDE CERAMIC POT
36 IN. LONG ½ IN. DOWEL ROD
8 IN. WIDE GREEN FOAM IN A CONE SHAPE
2 CASES ASPARAGUS (12 LB.)
1 BOX OF U-PICKS (GREENING PINS)
12 ROSES
SHEET MOSS

Using a prepared mix, pour plaster of paris into a ceramic pot. Insert a dowel rod into the center of the wet plaster and hold until it sets. Once the plaster fully sets (about 20 minutes), attach the tree-shaped foam cone tightly over the dowel rod.

Starting 3 inches from the foam tree top, attach each asparagus spear with a u-pick. Place the spears together tightly, one layer at a time. The picks should be placed toward the base of each spear. For one person, this could take roughly two hours. The next step is to drape the sheet moss around the bottom of the tree to cover the dowel rod from view. (You can place the tree into a decorative urn.)

The rose cluster (or artichokes) crowning the topiary is usually assembled at the event, to assure freshness. Using a dozen cut roses (and baby's breath), attach them to the top and sides using u-picks on the stems.

Figs and Prosciutto

Serves 12

Very easy. This makes a good presentation on a buffet table.

24 FRESH BLACK MISSION FIGS
2 POUNDS PROSCIUTTO, VERY THINLY SLICED
12 OUNCES FRESH GOAT CHEESE

Slice the figs in half and arrange on a silver tray with the prosciutto in the middle. Sprinkle the figs with goat cheese. ✒

Tomato Sandwiches

Serves 20

This recipe is simple, but so successful. I actually have guests coming into the kitchen at parties asking me where the sandwiches are. I see a lot of disappointed faces when I have to tell them the client did not order them for that night.

8 RIPE TOMATOES, IN SEASON
80 SLICES WHITE SANDWICH BREAD
3 CUPS MAYONNAISE
2 TABLESPOONS LAWRY'S SEASONED SALT

Peel the tomatoes by first cutting an X across the bottoms, then dipping in boiling water until the skins pop (about 1 minute). Slice each to yield 5 slices. Put the slices on a tray between paper towels and refrigerate them overnight to drain.

Cut the bread into rounds with a 3-inch biscuit cutter. Mix together the mayonnaise and seasoned salt in a small bowl until evenly combined.

Spread bread rounds with the mayonnaise mixture, place a tomato slice on one piece of bread, and close with the other. Repeat until all the bread rounds and tomato slices are used. Arrange on a serving tray lined with doilies. ✒

Ham Sweet Potato Biscuits

Serves 36

¼ CUP LIGHTLY MASHED COOKED SWEET POTATOES

⅔ CUP MILK

¼ CUP BUTTER, MELTED

1¼ CUPS ALL-PURPOSE FLOUR, SIFTED

1 TABLESPOON SUGAR

4 TEASPOONS BAKING POWDER

½ TEASPOON SALT

1 POUND COUNTRY HAM, THINLY SLICED

Cranberry Mayonnaise

1 CUP MAYONNAISE

½ (14.5-OUNCE) CAN JELLED CRANBERRY SAUCE

I love the combination of sweet potato biscuits with salted country ham and cranberry mayonnaise.

Preheat the oven to 450° F. Lightly grease a large baking sheet.

Combine the sweet potatoes, milk, and butter in large mixing bowl. Sift together the flour, sugar, baking powder, and salt into the potato mixture. Mix to form a soft dough.

Knead the dough until smooth on a lightly floured surface. Roll out to a thickness of ½ inch and cut with a 2-inch biscuit cutter. Place on the prepared baking sheet. Each biscuit should touch another.

Bake for 8 to 10 minutes, until golden brown. Let them cool on baking sheet.

To make the cranberry mayonnaise, put mayonnaise and cranberry sauce in food processor and process until smooth.

Spread the cranberry mayonnaise on biscuits, fill with ham, and wrap in foil, making two layers of biscuits. You may store them overnight in refrigerator. Warm at 350° F for 15 minutes if the biscuits are at room temperature or 25 to 30 minutes if they have been refrigerated. ⇾

Oyster Stew

Serves 4

A very elegant stew for a winter cocktail party. I played with this stew for a long time before I got it right. Cooking down the liquids to make a creamy sauce is the trick.

1 PINT SHUCKED OYSTERS (RESERVE LIQUID)
6 TABLESPOONS UNSALTED BUTTER
1 CELERY STALK, FINELY CHOPPED
½ ONION, FINELY CHOPPED
2 CUPS WHIPPING CREAM
2 CUPS HALF-AND-HALF
SALT AND FRESHLY GROUND BLACK PEPPER
2 TABLESPOONS DRY SHERRY

Pick through the oysters for shells. Reserve the liquid.

Heat the butter in a medium saucepan over medium heat. Add the celery and sauté briefly, 1 minute. Add the onion and sauté until limp, 5 minutes. Add the oysters and sauté until the edges curl. With a slotted spoon, transfer the oysters to a plate.

Add the cream, half-and-half, and reserved oyster liquid. Cook down to about 3 cups total liquid over medium heat, about 10 minutes.

Return the oysters to the saucepan. Add salt and pepper and the sherry. Serve hot. ⤳

Leg of Lamb with Chutney Butter

Serves 6

I met Craig Claiborne, former New York Times *food critic, in East Hampton a couple of years before he died. He invited my mother, sisters, and me to his house for drinks. He was a true Southern gentleman. This is the way he cooked his leg of lamb.*

5-POUND LEG OF LAMB, TRIMMED (BONE-IN)
1 CLOVE GARLIC, SLICED
1 TEASPOON FRESH ROSEMARY
FRESH LEMON JUICE
SALT AND FRESHLY GROUND BLACK PEPPER

Chutney Butter
1 POUND UNSALTED BUTTER
1 CUP GOOD-QUALITY CHUTNEY

Preheat the oven to 300° F.

Cut small slits in the lamb and insert the garlic. Rub the meat with rosemary and lemon juice and sprinkle with salt and pepper.

Place the meat on a rack in a roasting pan and roast, uncovered, for 18 minutes per pound for well done (175° F on a meat thermometer), 12 minutes per pound for rare (140° F).

Transfer the lamb to a warm serving tray and let stand for 20 minutes before carving.

To make the chutney butter, combine the butter and chutney in a food processor. Process together until blended.

Slice the lamb thinly and serve the chutney butter on the side. ⸙

Marinated Lamb Chops with Mint Sauce

Serves 20

5 CUPS RED WINE

2½ CUPS EXTRA VIRGIN OLIVE OIL

1¼ CUPS HONEY

½ CUP PLUS 1 TABLESPOON SOY SAUCE

2½ TABLESPOONS DRIED THYME

2½ TABLESPOONS DRIED ROSEMARY

2½ TABLESPOONS MINCED FRESH GINGER

1½ TABLESPOONS PLUS ½ TEASPOON MINCED GARLIC

SALT AND FRESHLY GROUND BLACK PEPPER

8 RACKS BABY LAMB CHOPS (8 CHOPS EACH)

Mint Sauce

1 CUP MINT JELLY

¾ CUP APPLE CIDER VINEGAR

¾ CUP WATER

2 TABLESPOONS CHOPPED FRESH MINT LEAVES

2 SHALLOTS, FINELY CHOPPED

SALT AND FRESHLY GROUND BLACK PEPPER

I marinate these overnight and grill them at cocktail parties. They are served as single chops. You need a stick to beat the men away from this station! Delicious!

Mix the wine, olive oil, honey, soy sauce, thyme, rosemary, ginger, and garlic in a nonreactive container. Season with salt and pepper. Add the lamb racks and marinate the meat overnight in the refrigerator.

The sauce can be made ahead and left out until needed. Mix together the mint jelly, vinegar, water, mint leaves, and shallots in a small saucepan. Heat over medium-low heat, stirring until the jelly melts. Season to taste with salt and pepper.

Prepare a hot fire in the grill.

Remove the lamb racks from marinade and grill, turning often, for 10 to 15 minutes or to an internal temperature of 130° F.

Slice into single chops and place on a platter. Serve with the mint sauce in a bowl in the middle of the platter. ⇘

Dining, Damask, and Demitasse

WHEN PEOPLE FIRST CALL ME THEY PRETTY MUCH KNOW THEY
WANT TO USE ME TO CATER FOR THEIR PARTY. THE REST
IS JUST NEGOTIATION ABOUT THE MENU AND THE BUDGET.
This is particularly true for dinner parties, which in many ways are more varied and more
complicated than less formal entertaining or cocktail parties. Whether I am asked to do a
seated or buffet dinner, the client usually has some special requests. When they don't
know what they want, I ask them what their favorite foods are, and we start from there.
The number of people, the relative formality of the event, and the budget determine
whether we do a seated dinner or not. People always enjoy being served, and several
courses are difficult for a buffet, so I usually suggest that smaller dinner parties at home
be seated affairs. These parties are more relaxed and conducive to conversation. Savannah
has a number of beautiful inns, where elegant dinner parties can be staged in a homey
atmosphere. Recently, I catered such a party at the Rhett House Inn in nearby Beaufort,
South Carolina. The hosts requested that we serve Carolina Gold rice.

Carolina Gold rice—named for its golden color in the field—has superior cooking
qualities, aroma, flavor, and texture. From 1750 to 1850 hundreds of miles of wetlands
were planted with Carolina Gold, but production almost disappeared after the Civil War.

Fortunately, in the mid 1980s, Dr. Richard Schulz from Savannah collected stores of Carolina Gold rice from a USDA seed bank and began production on a plantation in Bluffton. Today the luscious Carolina Gold rice is once again readily available from Anson Mills.

In the 18th and 19th centuries, several cultural traditions in the Low Country—Italian, French Huguenot, English, African, and Native American—produced regional recipes, some of which have been handed down

for generations. Italian and African influences combined to make the dish I served at the Rhett House. Originally called *reezy peezy* (Gullah) or *rici e bisi* (Italian), the recipe calls for Carolina Gold rice, fresh peas, and mint and is now sometimes called *reetzi beetzi*.

When people imagine Savannah, they think of historic townhouses filled with antiques. But some Savannahians live with striking contemporary interiors. One such client lives in the penthouse of the old C & S Bank Building with panoramic views of the city, including our beautiful new bridge over the Savannah River, the spires of St. John the Baptist Cathedral, First Presbyterian Church, and St. John's Episcopal Church, and interesting rooftops and treetops. Their Southwestern art collection and modern furniture is captivating, and fortunately they love to entertain. Once I opened a cabinet and found the most beautiful bowls I have ever seen. When I

breathlessly asked, "What are these?" Lorelei said, "Oh, those are some Steuben bowls we got as a wedding present." Every party I have done for them since, I have insisted on using those bowls, except, obviously, for their daughter's huge wedding. That was one of the biggest and most beautiful weddings ever held in Savannah. Ann married Tom Lee, the venture capitalist, art collector, and philanthropist from Boston and New York, in Forsyth Park at sunset amid the park's renowned fountain and flowers.

Tom and Ann have flown my staff and me up to New York several times to cater "Savannah" parties for them. The most memorable was for Wynton Marsalis. Tom is very involved with Lincoln Center, so when he and Ann hosted a benefit dinner for Jazz at Lincoln Center, they asked me to do the food. I took two of my cooks, Annette and her sister Vanessa, with me, and we had a ball touring around New York. At the end of the dinner, Wynton stood up to thank everyone, and he asked me to come out and bragged on my food, especially the corn pudding *(Corn Pudding, page 139)*. I was thrilled to get a standing ovation. ❧

Recipes

Yellow Tomato Gazpacho

Serves 8

I have been making gazpacho for years using red tomatoes. This is a wonderful change from the red tomatoes and a wonderful color especially when you garnish with crème fraîche and avocados. I love to garnish this with a lobster tail when I can.

5 POUNDS FRESH YELLOW TOMATOES, CORED AND CHOPPED

½ CUCUMBER, PEELED, SEEDED, AND CHOPPED

2 STALKS CELERY, CHOPPED

1 YELLOW BELL PEPPER, SEEDED AND CHOPPED

½ JALAPEÑO PEPPER, SEEDED AND CHOPPED

½ VIDALIA ONION, CHOPPED

½ TEASPOON MINCED FRESH GARLIC

1 TABLESPOON FRESH LEMON JUICE

1 TABLESPOON CHAMPAGNE VINEGAR OR OTHER WHITE WINE VINEGAR

3 TABLESPOONS EXTRA VIRGIN OLIVE OIL

½ TEASPOON LOUISIANA HOT SAUCE

1¼ TEASPOONS SUGAR

½ TEASPOON GROUND CUMIN

½ TEASPOON CELERY SALT

SALT AND FRESHLY GROUND BLACK PEPPER

8 TO 10 TABLESPOONS CRÈME FRAÎCHE, FOR GARNISH

4 AVOCADOS, PEELED AND SLICED, FOR GARNISH

Combine the tomatoes, cucumber, celery, bell pepper, jalapeño, and onion in a food processor and puree. Refrigerate until well chilled.

Add the garlic, lemon juice and vinegar and mix well. Then add the cumin, celery salt, oil, hot sauce, sugar, salt, and pepper. Refrigerate until the mixture is cold and ready to serve.

Garnish each serving with a dollop of crème fraîche and fanned out avocado slices. ⇝

Tomato Bisque

Serves 8 to 10

4 ounces bacon

2 onions, finely chopped

6 celery stalks, finely chopped

1 bay leaf

1 teaspoon fresh thyme

4 large cloves garlic, finely chopped

1 (28-ounce) can diced tomatoes (reserve the juice)

1 (6-ounce) can tomato paste

2 tablespoons (¼ stick) unsalted butter

3 tablespoons all-purpose flour

4 cups whipping cream, at room temperature

Salt and freshly ground black pepper

1 small bunch of basil, for garnish

I saw this soup recipe in a food magazine twenty years ago. It was from a hotel in Houston, Texas. Over the years, I lost the second half of the magazine page, so I improvise. I think I improvise pretty well.

Fry the bacon in large skillet over medium-high heat until the fat is rendered, about 8 minutes (depending on bacon thickness); remove the bacon (and use as desired). Add onions, celery, bay leaf, and thyme to the bacon grease and sauté until the onions are translucent, about 7 minutes. Add the garlic and sauté over medium-high heat until very lightly browned. Add the tomatoes with juice and tomato paste and bring to boil, stirring occasionally. Lower the heat, cover, and simmer for 30 minutes.

Melt the butter in a large saucepan over medium-high heat. Add the flour and whisk to form a paste. Cook while stirring for 5 minutes. Slowly add the cream and continue cooking until thickened.

Remove the bay leaf from the tomatoes and add the cream mixture to the simmering tomato mixture, stirring until thickened. Season with salt and pepper. Serve hot, garnishing each serving with a basil leaf. ⇌

Reetzi Beetzi (Rice and Peas)

Serves 6

3 tablespoons unsalted butter
1 yellow onion, finely chopped
1 (10-ounce) bag frozen peas
Pinch of salt or more to taste
1 cup chicken broth
2 cups water
1 cup arborio rice
2 tablespoons chopped fresh flat-leaf parsley
Freshly grated Parmigiano-Reggiano

A nice way to combine rice and vegetables, this goes well with any chicken or seafood dish.

Melt the butter in a medium saucepan over medium heat. Add the onion and sauté until limp, about 5 minutes. Add the peas and salt, and cook, stirring constantly, for 2 minutes. Add the broth and water and bring to a boil. Stir in the rice and parsley, decrease the heat to medium-low, cover, and cook, stirring occasionally, until the rice is al dente and the peas are very soft, about 20 minutes.

Adjust the seasonings and serve immediately before the rice absorbs any more liquid. Top with grated Parmigiano-Reggiano, if desired. ⚘

Mother's Potatoes

Serves 8 to 10

8 to 10 medium white potatoes, peeled and thinly sliced
½ cup (1 stick) unsalted butter, cut into 1-tablespoon pats
3 tablespoons all-purpose flour
Salt and white pepper
4½ cups whole milk
1 cup grated Gruyère cheese

I grew up on these potatoes, and they still say home to me. This makes a good buffet dish.

Preheat the oven to 375° F.

Layer the potatoes in a 9 by 13-inch casserole dish. Over each layer, dot with butter and lightly sprinkle with flour, salt, and white pepper. You should use three layers for a 9 by 13-inch dish. Finish by pouring the milk to cover all the layers.

Bake, uncovered, until potatoes are done, approximately 1 hour. Remove from oven and sprinkle with the cheese. Return to the oven to melt the cheese, 5 to 10 minutes. Serve hot. ⚘

Pickled Shrimp

Serves 8 to 10

When I was growing up in Dothan, Alabama, I had a boyfriend named Tim Harrison whose mother, Dot, was a fabulous cook. My family still talks about Dot's greens beans, but my favorite was her pickled shrimp.

$2\frac{1}{2}$ POUNDS (21 TO 26) LARGE SHRIMP, PEELED, DEVEINED, TAILS REMOVED

2 STALKS CELERY, CHOPPED

$\frac{1}{2}$ CUP SLICED ONION RINGS

$1\frac{1}{2}$ CUPS CHOPPED GREEN BELL PEPPER

$1\frac{1}{4}$ CUPS VEGETABLE OIL

$\frac{3}{4}$ CUP APPLE CIDER VINEGAR

$1\frac{1}{2}$ TEASPOONS SALT

7 OR 8 BAY LEAVES

$2\frac{1}{2}$ TABLESPOONS CAPERS AND JUICE

6 TO 7 DROPS TABASCO SAUCE

Bring a large pot of salted water to a boil, drop the shrimp in, and reduce to a simmer. Cook the shrimp in simmering water for 3 to 5 minutes, until pink. Drain well.

In 2-quart glass container, combine the shrimp, celery, onion, bell peppers, oil, vinegar, salt, bay leaves, capers and juice, and Tabasco. Cover and chill for 24 hours stirring occasionally.

Drain the liquid before serving and remove the bay leaves. Serve with party picks or as a buffet dish. ✒

Jumbo Lump Crabmeat with Pink Sauce

Serves 8

This is an excellent first course. I think the color and taste of the sauce are wonderful.

Pink Sauce
2 CUPS MAYONNAISE
½ CUP KETCHUP
¼ CUP BRANDY

8 TO 10 OUNCES MESCLUN GREENS
1 POUND JUMBO LUMP CRABMEAT, DRAINED
100 TOAST POINTS (see recipe on page 116)

Make the pink sauce by combining the mayonnaise, ketchup, and brandy in a small bowl and mixing well.

Arrange a bed of greens on a platter. Mound the crab on the greens and pour the pink sauce on the top.

Serve with toast points. ⋟

Catering Tips ❧ Silver Collections

For many Southerners when we hear the word "silver," it evokes memories of the beautiful heirlooms our mothers and grandmothers would lovingly use with pride on special occasions. Laboriously polishing each time-honored heirloom to a gleaming patina was the right of passage for many young people. Silver on the Southern table has long been a source of pride, civility, and graciousness unequalled by any other component; allowing silver to become a social icon early in Southern history, thus transcending even modern decorative trends. There is nothing like old silver to warm a room and add instant refinement to any interior. The use of

silver has long since set the standard of elegance and refinement for the Southern table.

Silver has always played an important role in entertaining in the South. Many of the settlers came from England and were accustomed to using fine silver. The first silversmith to come to Georgia was Will Parker, who arrived in Savannah on August 29, 1733, just seven months after the colony was established. There are no surviving pieces attributed to him, but we know that he was an English-trained silversmith.

Frederick Marquand is probably the best-known Savannah silversmith. The most numerous identifiable surviving pieces bear his hallmark. Over two hundred pieces of silver with identifiable marks of fifty-eight craftsmen and firms operating in Georgia between 1790 and 1870 were exhibited at the High Museum of Art in Atlanta (Georgia Collects: American Silver, 1780–1870).

American silver during this early period was made from melted-down coins (thus, the term "coin silver"), a practice

I REALLY ENJOY LOOKING AT MY CLIENTS' COLLECTIONS OF SILVER. MANY HAVE BEAUTIFUL PIECES THAT THEY HAVE INHERITED OR COLLECTED OVER THE YEARS. I LOVE TO OPEN THE DRAWERS AND PICK OUT PIECES TO USE FOR THE PARTY.

that was illegal in England. There were several reasons for this practice: (1) It was more convenient—silver bars were difficult to import; (2) It was safer—there were no banks during this time and a silver service bearing the maker's marks and the owner's monogram was much easier to identify, if stolen, than a bag of coins.

Beef Tenderloin with Madeira Sauce

Serves 6 to 8

5- TO 6-POUND TENDERLOIN, OVEN READY (TRIMMED
BUT NOT TIED)
MORTON NATURE'S SEASONS SEASONING BLEND

Madeira Sauce
3 TABLESPOONS UNSALTED BUTTER
3 TABLESPOONS ALL-PURPOSE FLOUR
½ CUP MADEIRA
2 (10.5-OUNCE) CANS BEEF BROTH

I have probably cooked five thousand tenderloins in my career, but I always use an instant-read thermometer to make sure it is at the right temperature. All of my staff carry meat thermometers in their pockets or purses at all times.

Many is the time I have wished that I had bought stock in Morton Salt because of their Nature's Seasons Seasoning Blend. I put it on everything but ice cream!

Preheat the oven to 400° F.

Sprinkle the meat with the seasoning blend and put in a large roasting pan. Roast for 20 minutes. Turn the meat over and roast for another 20 minutes, until the meat registers 120° F on an instant-read thermometer for rare.

While the meat roasts, make the sauce. Melt the butter in a medium saucepan over medium heat. Add the flour and whisk until you have a paste. Add the Madeira and broth and cook, stirring, until thick.

Let the meat sit before carving. Then serve together the beef tenderloin and warm sauce. The sauce can be made a day ahead and warmed before serving. ⇝

Pears Stuffed with Roquefort and Walnuts in Pastry

Serves 4

¼ cup crumbled ROQUEFORT OR OTHER CRUMBLY BLUE CHEESE (3½ OUNCES), CHILLED
6 TABLESPOONS FRESH BREAD CRUMBS, LIGHTLY TOASTED AND COOLED
⅓ CUP CHOPPED WALNUTS (1 OUNCE), TOASTED AND FINELY CHOPPED
4 SMALL FIRM-RIPE ANJOU PEARS, WITH STEMS
1 SLICE FIRM WHITE SANDWICH BREAD
1 SHEET FROZEN PUFF PASTRY (8 OUNCES), THAWED
1 LARGE EGG, LIGHTLY BEATEN

This could be placed on a bed of baby greens and served as a cheese and fruit course.

Combine the cheese, bread crumbs, and walnuts. Mash with a fork. Cover the mixture with plastic wrap and freeze just until firm, about 10 minutes.

Scoop out the center of the bottom of each pear with the large end of a melon-baller. Then continue to remove the core to make a ¼-cup cavity. Fill each cavity evenly with the cheese mixture and seal the bottom with a small piece of bread.

Butter a large 1-inch-deep baking pan.

On a lightly floured surface with a floured rolling pin, roll out the pastry to a thickness of ¹⁄₁₆ inch to form a 15-inch square. Cut the dough into quarters to make four equal pieces.

Stand 1 pear in center of a pastry square. Brush the pear all over with the egg. Bring one corner of the pastry up toward the top of the pear, pressing it against the pear to adhere. Repeat with adjacent corner, then generously brush the pastry with egg before pressing closely against side of pear. Repeat the process with the remaining two corners. Fold the top points of the pastry ¼ inch down and brush with egg. Do not cover the stem. Transfer the wrapped pear to the prepared baking pan and chill while wrapping the remaining pears. Place the pears 5 inches apart in the baking pan. Chill the wrapped pears for 30 minutes.

Preheat the oven to 425° F.

Bake the pears on the middle oven rack for 20 minutes, or until fruit is just tender when pierced with a knife and pastry is golden and cooked through. (There will be some minor shrinkage, but the pastry will be puffed.)

Let the pears cool in the pan for at least 15 minutes before serving. ⸙

Coconut Pound Cake

Serves 12

This cake is a variation of Mrs. Joseph's pound cake. Mrs. Joseph's daughter was a friend of mine when I was a child. Mrs. Joseph would often pick me up to spend the night. Getting in the car with Mrs. Joseph was very dangerous because she was a terrible driver, but she was a great cook. The cake was almost worth the ride!

This cake has a nice macaroon–like top. It slices better the day after it is baked. It will keep nicely in the refrigerator for several days and also freezes well.

6 LARGE EGGS

1 CUP CRISCO

½ CUP UNSALTED BUTTER, AT ROOM TEMPERATURE

3 CUPS SUGAR

½ TEASPOON ALMOND EXTRACT

½ TEASPOON COCONUT EXTRACT

3 CUPS SIFTED CAKE FLOUR

1 CUP MILK

2 CUPS PACKAGED OR FRESH FLAKED COCONUT

Preheat the oven to 300° F. Grease and flour a 10-inch tube pan.

Separate the eggs. Set the whites aside and allow to come to room temperature. Beat the egg yolks with the Crisco and butter at high speed until well blended. Gradually add the sugar, beating until light and fluffy. Add the extracts and beat. At low speed, beat in the flour (about one-quarter at a time), alternating with the milk (about one-third at a time). Begin and end with the flour. Add the coconut and beat on medium speed until well blended.

In a clean bowl, beat the egg whites until stiff peaks form. Gently fold the whites into the batter. Pour into the prepared pan.

Bake for 2 hours.

Cool the cake in the pan on a wire rack for 15 minutes. Remove from the pan and finish cooling on a rack. ⇁

FESTIVALS, FIREWORKS, AND FRIENDS

I HAVE A GOOD FRIEND WHO RENTS A HOUSE EVERY JUNE IN THE SOUTH OF FRANCE NEAR RAMATUELLE. For the last ten years I've spent a week or more with her, and all we do is comb the markets and cook. Now Jane and I know all the important people in San Tropez—the butcher, the baker, the cheese man, the fishmonger, and the flower cart lady. We throw several dinner parties, where we set the table for ten out on the terrace and decorate with flowers from the gardens. Of course the wine begins to flow the minute we begin cooking. We always drink the local rosé, which is the summer choice of the French. Jane and I cook together, and we fight together because we are very competitive in the kitchen, but somehow we present a beautiful dinner every time. I've gotten three marriage proposals for my macaroni and cheese, which I developed for one of these French fêtes. Back in Savannah at my fancy parties, I could call it "gratin de macaroni a l'ancienne." I served my macaroni and cheese at Helen's Fourth of July party, but apparently American men don't propose marriage over great food the way Frenchmen do.

It is always fun to do holiday parties when special foods and decorations are in order. At Christmastime I do vegetable wreaths. I cover a wreath form with parsley, then cut crudités, such as radishes and squashes, into different shapes and put them on the wreath with tooth picks. The wreath really does look like something you'd hang on your door, but it's all edible. I put it on a big round silver tray, and it looks beautiful. Once I did two topiary cranberry trees as the center piece on a dining room table and used straight pins to put the cranberries on the tree form. They were really beautiful and Christmassy with a bright silver center in each vibrant red cranberry, but my fingers bled for days.

One of the prettiest Christmas tablecloths I've ever done was made out of shiny, green galax leaves from North Carolina. I hot-glued the leaves all over a burlap tablecloth, and the way it folded and draped was just gorgeous. I try to use traditional holiday colors, so my red velvet cake *(Red Velvet Cake, page 60)* is the most asked for dessert during December. Of course I slip it in for Fourth of July parties and Valentine's Day, too. Virginia hams are also popular for Christmas cocktail parties. I always buy two, cut one up and arrange all the slices around the whole ham. That makes for a lavish presentation.

People in Savannah love rice, so I do a lot of rice recipes. Harriet's rice, which I serve all year-round, is great for large gatherings because it always comes out perfectly. But it reminds me of Christmas every time I make it. My friend Haidee's mother, whose name is Harriet, calls me every Christmas from Spartanburg and asks me how I make my rice. I tell her and then remind her that she taught me how to make it twenty years ago—so I call it Harriet's rice *(Harriet's Oven Cooked Rice, page 144)*.

Of all the holiday parties I do, the most extravagant and unusual is the Midnight in the Garden party SCAD puts on every Halloween night in Bonaventure Cemetery. The SCAD Film Festival is at the end of October. Bobby Zarem says that he doesn't have any trouble getting movie stars, producers, and directors to come down here for the festival because they are treated so well, and the Midnight in the Garden party is the highlight. We work out of tents practically in the dark. Because there is no electricity, everything we serve is cold.

One New Year's Eve I did a seated dinner for 350 people at the Telfair for the Century Club, which is a local men's club. Very Southern. I was worried about getting enough help on New Year's Eve for that many people, so I started putting the word out that I would pay twenty dollars per hour cash the night of the party. I told everyone who signed up to bring a friend to work, too, and I just told my friend John Tatum, the governor of the club, that I didn't know who would show up, but we had to pay them. On the night of the party they started coming in and a lot of them looked like they had just gotten off a roadwork gang—straggle-haired, huge gold necklaces, white tennis shoes, and I don't know what all. I lined them up and stood there and said, "Kitchen, waiter, waiter, kitchen, etc.," as they filed by. We ended up with enough people to serve the tables, but I watched everything like a hawk. Across the room I saw the very distinguished head of the Mercedes dealership pouring wine, so I rushed over and asked, "Dale, what are you doing pouring wine?"

"Well, that young man came over to me and said, 'Sir, I've never poured wine before, would you show me how to do it?'" After that I thought everything went just fine. The food got to the tables hot, and nobody dropped a tray. It was only the next day that I learned one of my new waiters leaned over to Bill Haile, president of SunTrust Bank, and said, "Man, ain't this one hell of a party!" So we pulled it off, but those are the kinds of things that happen in my business that keep it from ever being a boring job! Happy New Year! ❧

Recipes

Chilled Corn Soup

Serves 8

16 EARS FRESH YELLOW CORN, HUSKED AND CLEANED

8 CUPS CHICKEN BROTH

3 CUPS WHOLE MILK

2 TABLESPOONS EXTRA VIRGIN OLIVE OIL

2 MEDIUM YELLOW ONIONS, THINLY SLICED

1 MEDIUM LEEK, WHITE AND LIGHT GREEN PARTS
ONLY, THINLY SLICED, RINSED WELL AND DRAINED

1 STALK CELERY, THINLY SLICED

2 SPRIGS THYME

1 CLOVE GARLIC, PEELED BUT LEFT WHOLE

SALT AND FRESHLY GROUND WHITE PEPPER

8 DROPS TABASCO SAUCE

8 (1¼-POUND) LOBSTERS

CHOPPED FRESH CHIVES, TO GARNISH

This is a wonderful soup to make in the summer, when corn is at its freshest. I first had a chilled corn soup in one of my favorite restaurants in the Hamptons. Of course, the corn you get in the Hamptons is like no other. Georgia corn is a close second. I love to serve this with a lobster garnish. Your local fishmonger or grocery store will steam and crack the tail for you. This saves a lot of trouble.

Using a sharp knife, slice the corn kernels off the cobs and set aside.

Combine the cobs, broth, and milk in a large pot and bring to a boil. Decrease the heat and simmer for 15 minutes. Remove and discard the cobs.

While the mixture is simmering, warm the olive oil in a medium pot over medium-low heat. Add the onions, leek, celery, thyme, and garlic. Season with salt and white pepper. Sauté, stirring frequently, until vegetables are translucent and tender, 8 to 10 minutes. Add the reserved corn and continue to cook for 3 to 5 minutes, until the corn is just softened.

Add the stock and milk mixture and bring to a boil. Decrease the heat and simmer for 20 minutes, skimming the surface to remove any foam. Remove and discard the thyme sprigs and garlic clove and transfer the soup to a blender. Puree until smooth. Add the Tabasco and season to taste with salt and white pepper.

Strain through a fine-mesh sieve. Cool the soup to room temperature, cover, and chill overnight.

To cook the lobsters, bring 2 inches of water to a boil in a 5-gallon steamer with a rack insert and tight-fitting cover. Add live lobster, cover and steam for 13 minutes. Remove the lobster and let cool. Use a nutcracker to crack the claws and tail and pull the meat out in one piece. Chill the meat overnight.

To serve, garnish each bowl with a tail, two claws, and a sprinkling of chives. ⸙

Three Pepper Soup

Serves 8

Pot I

½ cup (1 stick) unsalted butter
4 red bell peppers, chopped
3 small white potatoes, peeled and diced
4 (10-ounce) cans chicken broth
2 cups whipping cream

Pot II

½ cup (1 stick) unsalted butter
4 green bell peppers, chopped
3 small white potatoes, peeled and diced
4 (10-ounce) cans chicken broth
2 cups whipping cream
Green food coloring

Pot III

½ cup (1 stick) unsalted butter
4 yellow bell peppers, chopped
3 small white potatoes, peeled and diced
4 (10-ounce cans) chicken broth
2 cups whipping cream

My friend Diana Barrow had this soup in a Washington, D.C., restaurant about ten years ago. She was very impressed with the presentation and taste. So we set about to recreate it for her. Don't be disheartened about all the steps, it is well worth the effort. It is very beautiful when served in Steuben soup bowls, but any old bowls will do.

Melt ½ cup butter in each of the three saucepans over medium-high heat. Add red peppers to pot I, green peppers to pot II, and yellow peppers to pot III. Sauté the peppers until limp. Add the potatoes and chicken broth to each pot and bring to a boil. Cook at a low boil until the potatoes are done (easily pierced with a fork), about 15 minutes.

Put each mixture in a food processor, one pot at a time. Process until smooth. Return each batch to its saucepan.

Add whipping cream to each mixture. Add a little green food coloring to the green pepper mixture. Refrigerate the three mixtures, separately, until cold.

When you are ready to serve, you will need assistance. Pour all three mixtures into each soup bowl at the same time, and it will automatically divide into three triangles. It's a Wow! ⤳

Curried Pumpkin Soup

Serves 6

¼ cup (½ stick) unsalted butter

1 large white onion, sliced

¾ cup sliced green onions (scallions), white part only

1 (16-ounce) can pumpkin puree

4 cups chicken broth

1 bay leaf

½ teaspoon sugar

¼ to ½ teaspoon curry powder

⅛ to ¼ teaspoon nutmeg

Few sprigs of parsley

2 cups whipping cream

Salt and freshly ground black pepper

Garnishes

½ cup whipping cream, whipped, sour cream, or yogurt

Paprika

½ cup minced chives or green onions (scallions)

When I first started my catering business, Martha Stewart came to town to lecture for the Junior League. I was asked to cater a lunch for her, and we served this soup out of a large pumpkin that I had bronzed in the oven. She seemed impressed. I serve this often in the fall as a first course in carved out small pumpkins. It is very labor-intensive but well worth the effort.

Melt the butter in a large saucepan over medium-high heat. Add the onions and sauté until soft and golden brown, about 7 minutes. Stir in the pumpkin, broth, bay leaf, sugar, curry powder, nutmeg, and parsley. Bring to a simmer, then lower the heat and continue simmering, uncovered, for 15 minutes, stirring occasionally. Remove the bay leaf.

Transfer the soup in batches to a blender or food processor and puree. Return to the saucepan and add the cream and salt and pepper to taste. Simmer for 5 to 10 minutes, but do not allow to boil.

To serve hot, ladle into individual bowls. Float a dollop of whipped cream on each and sprinkle with paprika. Top with chives. To serve cold, chill the soup thoroughly, then ladle into individual bowls.

Note: The soup may be refrigerated for up to 3 days or frozen for 3 months.

Watermelon, Arugula, and Pine Nut Salad

Serves 4

The combined flavors of sweet watermelon and bitter arugula just pop in your mouth. This is a great summer salad when watermelon is at its best. It looks beautiful on a buffet table.

1 tablespoon fresh lemon juice
1 tablespoon red wine vinegar
½ teaspoon salt or to taste
2 tablespoons extra virgin olive oil
3 cups cubed (½- to ¾-inch cubes) seeded watermelon
(from a 2 ½-pound piece, rind discarded)
6 cups baby arugula (6 ounces)
½ cup pine nuts (1 ounce)
⅓ cup crumbled feta or fresh goat cheese (1½ ounces)
Coarsely ground black pepper
Fleur de sel (optional)

Whisk together the lemon juice, vinegar, and salt in a large bowl. Add the oil in a slow stream, whisking until emulsified. Add the watermelon, arugula, and pine nuts and toss to coat. Sprinkle with the cheese, pepper, and fleur de sel (if using). Serve immediately. ⤳

Hot Crab Dip

Serves 5 to 6

This is an easy dish to make for a party. I serve it in a chafing dish along with toast points. The dip can be assembled ahead and reheated. I add crab just before serving.

1 LOAF THINLY SLICED SANDWICH BREAD
3 TABLESPOONS BUTTER
¼ CUP ONION, CHOPPED
2 TABLESPOONS ALL-PURPOSE FLOUR
1 CUP HALF-AND-HALF
½ CUP MAYONNAISE
1 CUP GRATED CHEDDAR CHEESE
¼ TEASPOON SALT
¼ TEASPOON PEPPER
2 TABLESPOONS DRY SHERRY
1 POUND WHITE CRABMEAT

First make the toast points. Preheat the oven to 200° F.

Cut the crusts from the bread slices and cut each into 4 triangles. Arrange in a single layer on a baking sheet and bake for about 1 hour, until dry and crispy.

Increase the oven temperature to 350° F. Butter a 1½-quart casserole dish.

Melt the butter in a medium saucepan over medium-high heat. Add the onion and sauté until translucent, about 7 minutes. Add the flour and stir to form a smooth paste. Pour in the half-and-half and heat, stirring constantly. As soon as mixture thickens, take off the burner. Add the mayonnaise and cheese and stir. Add the salt, pepper, sherry, and crabmeat and stir to blend. Turn into the prepared casserole.

Bake for 45 minutes or until bubbly. Serve hot with the toast points. ⤳

The thing that strikes everyone about the Strawberry Tree is how it fills the room with a sweet aroma. People are drawn to it like bees to a flower!

Catering Tips ⇒ Strawberry Tree

Plaster of paris
8 in. wide ceramic pot
36 in. long ½ in. dowel rod
8 in. wide green foam in a cone shape
2 flats of strawberries (12 pints)
1 box (250 count) toothpicks with cellophane
12 roses
1 box u-picks (greening pins)
Sheet moss

Using a prepared mix (found at craft stores), pour plaster of paris into a ceramic pot. Insert a dowel rod into the center of the wet plaster and hold until it sets. Once the plaster fully sets (about 20 minutes), attach the tree-shaped foam cone tightly over the dowel rod.

Starting at the bottom of the tree, begin attaching strawberries in tight rows, one layer at a time. Insert a toothpick through the center of each strawberry, with the green leafy part against the form. This goes faster with several people, so give yourself a couple of hours if tackling the project on your own.

As you near the top, leave about 3 inches for the rose cluster. For this, use a dozen cut roses (and baby's breath), attaching them to the top and sides using u-picks on the stems. As a final touch, drape the fresh sheet moss so that it covers the dowel rod at the base of the tree. (You can also insert finished tree into an urn and add more greenery.)

Heirloom Tomato Tart

Serves 6

Try to make this when you can get heirloom tomatoes. I love the colors of green, red, purple, and yellow. I use Pillsbury refrigerated pie crust.

PREPARED UNSWEETENED PIE DOUGH FOR A SINGLE PIE
2½ TABLESPOONS EXTRA VIRGIN OLIVE OIL, PLUS MORE FOR DRIZZLING
2 ONIONS, THINLY SLICED
SALT AND FRESHLY GROUND BLACK PEPPER
1 CUP FRESH GOAT CHEESE
1 POUND TOMATOES (ANY COMBINATION OF RED, YELLOW, HEIRLOOM, CHERRY),
SLICED IF LARGE OR HALVED IF SMALL
½ CUP CRUMBLED FETA OR STILTON CHEESE
½ CUP PITTED KALAMATA OLIVES (OPTIONAL)
12 BASIL LEAVES, SLICED

Preheat the oven to 375° F.

Roll out the dough to a thickness of ¼ inch and line an 8-inch or 4 by 13-inch tart pan with it, pressing any excess dough against the sides to make a thicker edge. Prick the bottom and sides with a fork. Line with foil, fill with pie weights or dried beans, and bake for 20 minutes. Remove the weights and foil and bake for another 7 to 8 minutes until the crust is golden brown. Let cool.

Heat the olive oil in a large skillet over medium heat. Add the onions, season with salt and pepper, and sauté until the onions are lightly browned, about 7 minutes.

Spread the onions over bottom of the crust and dot with goat cheese. Arrange the tomatoes on top in a mosaic pattern. Dot with feta or Stilton and push olives into the top. Sprinkle lightly with salt and pepper and drizzle with olive oil.

Preheat the broiler. Cover the edge of the crust with foil to protect it from burning and broil until tart is lightly browned and bubbly, 4 to 5 minutes. Let cool to room temperature and garnish with basil. ⌇

Fried Green Tomatoes

Serves 8

When we have parties that have stations set up, this station has the second largest line. The crab cake station is always the longest, but this is a very popular one.

Chipotle Mayonnaise
1 cup mayonnaise
3 chipotles canned in adobo sauce, finely chopped
1 teaspoon adobo sauce

1 (10-ounce) box cornmeal
1 (10-ounce) box hush puppy mix
8 green tomatoes, sliced ¼ inch thick
½ to 1 cup vegetable oil, for frying
½ to 1 cup bacon grease, for frying
Sugar

First, make the chipotle mayonnaise. Stir together the mayonnaise, chipotles, and adobo sauce until well combined. The sauce may be made 1 week ahead and stored in the refrigerator, covered.

Mix together the cornmeal and hush puppy mix in a brown paper bag. Add the tomatoes and shake to cover the tomatoes with the dry mix.

Fill a 12-inch skillet with ½ cup vegetable oil and ½ cup bacon grease (2 to 3 inches of oil and grease mixture). Add the tomatoes in batches of 5 slices and fry. Keep turning the tomatoes until golden brown. Drain on paper towels and keep warm as you continue to fry the tomatoes. Sprinkle the slices with sugar. Serve immediately with the chipotle mayonnaise. ☙

Black-Eyed Pea Vinaigrette

Serves 8 to 10

2 (16-ounce) cans black-eyed peas
1 small onion, minced
2 red bell peppers, diced
¼ cup minced fresh parsley
½ teaspoon dried dill weed or 1½ teaspoons minced fresh dill
¼ cup extra virgin olive oil
¼ cup red wine vinegar
Salt and freshly ground black pepper

I serve this vinaigrette along with tomato and corn salsa (below) as complements to my fried green tomatoes.

Rinse and drain the peas. Combine in a mixing bowl with the onion, peppers, parsley, and dill. Sprinkle with equal amounts of oil and vinegar, until well moistened. Add salt and pepper to taste. Marinate in the refrigerator for several hours. Serve at room temperature in a bowl. ☙

Tomato and Corn Salsa

Serves 10 to 12

¼ cup (½ stick) unsalted butter
2 (16-ounce) bags yellow frozen corn, thawed
2½ tablespoons sugar
10 tomatoes, chopped
½ red onion, chopped
½ cup red wine vinegar
Salt and freshly ground black pepper

Melt the butter in a large skillet over medium-high heat. Add the corn and sauté until heated through, about 20 minutes. Drain and transfer to a serving bowl. Add the sugar. Let cool.

Add the tomatoes, onion, vinegar, and salt and pepper to taste. Serve immediately or make ahead of time and store in refrigerator overnight. ☙

Fresh Basil Cheesecake

Serves 10 to 12

½ cup fresh bread crumbs

1¼ cups freshly grated Parmesan cheese

1 tablespoon unsalted butter

2½ cups packed fresh basil leaves, plus additional leaves, to garnish

½ cup fresh parsley leaves

¼ cup extra virgin olive oil

½ teaspoon salt

¼ teaspoon cayenne pepper

1 large clove garlic

2 cups ricotta cheese, at room temperature

4 (8-ounce) packages cream cheese, softened

5 large eggs

½ cup pine nuts

I like to serve this on a footed glass cake stand. I put crackers beside the dish and stand back. It is a hit, especially with men.

Preheat the oven to 350° F. Generously butter a 10-inch springform pan.

Mix the bread crumbs and ¼ cup Parmesan cheese in a small bowl. Sprinkle the mixture into the bottom of prepared pan.

In a food processor, combine the basil, parsley, oil, salt, cayenne, and garlic and process until a smooth paste forms.

In a mixing bowl, beat the ricotta, cream cheese, and remaining 1 cup Parmesan cheese until smooth and light, about 5 minutes. Scrape the sides of the bowl and add in the eggs, one at a time, and continue to beat for 2 minutes. Divide the mixture between two bowls, putting two-thirds of the mixture in one bowl and leaving one-third of the mixture in the original bowl.

Fold the basil mixture into the bowl containing two-thirds of the cheese mixture until well blended.

Pour the basil-cheese mixture into the prepared springform pan. Carefully spread the plain cheese mixture on top. Sprinkle with pine nuts.

Set the pan on baking sheet and bake for 1½ hours. Turn off the oven and cool the cheesecake in the oven for about 1 hour with the oven door slightly ajar.

Remove from the oven, loosen the sides of the springform pan, and remove the cheesecake. Cool completely on a wire rack. Serve at room temperature, garnished with basil. ✢

Old-Fashioned Baked Macaroni and Cheese

Serves 6

8 OUNCES ELBOW MACARONI
7 OUNCES THINLY SLICED PROSCIUTTO
3 OUNCES BACON, CUT INTO STRIPS
1½ CUPS CRÈME FRAÎCHE
2 CUPS HEAVY WHIPPING CREAM
SALT AND FRESHLY GROUND BLACK PEPPER
2 TABLESPOONS FRESHLY GRATED PARMESAN CHEESE
1 CUP GRUYÈRE CHEESE, GRATED

This is a recipe I prepared in France and received three marriage proposals as a result. Be careful to whom you serve this!

Preheat the oven to 425° F. Butter a shallow ovenproof glass or earthenware 9 by 13-inch casserole dish.

Fry the bacon until crisp in a large skillet over medium heat, about 10 minutes, turning frequently. Drain on paper towels.

Cook the macaroni in plenty of salted boiling water until still quite firm. Drain. Return the macaroni to the pot and mix in the proscuitto, bacon, crème fraîche, and cream. Add salt and pepper to taste. Transfer to the prepared casserole. Sprinkle with the cheeses.

Bake for 25 minutes, until the cheese is browned on top and the liquid is completely absorbed.

Let sit for 5 minutes before serving. ❧

Squash Casserole

Serves 8 to 10

2 POUNDS YELLOW SUMMER SQUASH
½ WHITE ONION, CHOPPED
2 CUPS CHICKEN BROTH
⅓ CUP SOUR CREAM
1½ CUPS GRATED CHEDDAR CHEESE
1 LARGE EGG
3 TABLESPOONS BUTTER OR MARGARINE
1 TEASPOON SALT
FRESHLY GROUND BLACK PEPPER

This is a recipe my sister Cynthia Warrick gave me. I added onions and omitted bread crumbs from original recipe.

Preheat the oven to 350° F.

Combine the squash and onion with the broth in a medium saucepan. Bring to a boil then decrease the heat to medium and simmer for about 30 minutes until the squash is tender. Mash with a potato masher, then drain. Add the sour cream, 1 cup of the cheese, egg, butter, and salt and pepper to taste. Mix until well blended. Transfer the mixture to a 9 by 13-inch baking dish. Sprinkle the remaining ½ cup cheese on top. Bake for 30 to 35 minutes until bubbling. Serve hot. ❧

Mother's Pecan Pie

Serves 8

9-inch unbaked pie shell
3 large eggs
1 cup sugar
½ cup light corn syrup
6 tablespoons butter, melted
1 teaspoon vanilla extract
1 cup pecans, chopped, or pecan halves
Whipped cream and mint leaves, for garnish

Growing up in a large family in a Southern town, I never thought anything special about having pecan pie on a daily basis. Now when I serve my mother's pecan pie at parties, I get rave reviews! And everyone thinks it is very special.

Preheat the oven to 350° F.

Prick the unbaked pie crust with a fork. Bake for 10 minutes. Remove from the oven and set aside.

In mixing bowl, beat the eggs. Gradually beat in the sugar until light. Add the corn syrup, butter, and vanilla extract. Fold in the pecans. Pour the mixture into the pie shell.

Bake for 45 to 60 minutes, or until knife inserted in center comes out clean. Cool the pie until it has set. Garnish slices with whipped cream and mint leaves. ❧

Derby Pie

Serves 8

1 cup sugar
½ cup all-purpose flour
2 large eggs, lightly beaten
½ cup (1 stick) unsalted butter, melted and cooled
1 teaspoon vanilla extract
1 (6-ounce) package semi-sweet chocolate chips
1 cup pecans or walnuts, chopped
9-inch deep-dish pie shell
Whipped cream, to serve

This is a delicious pie, but it is ooh so rich!

Preheat the oven to 325° F.

Mix the sugar and flour in a large mixing bowl. Add the eggs, butter, vanilla, chocolate chips, and nuts. Mix well. Pour into the pie crust.

Bake for 1 hour, or until a tester inserted into the center of the pie comes out clean.

Cool the pie on a wire rack. Serve topped with a dollop of whipped cream. ❧

Blueberry Cheesecake Bars

Makes 24 bars

Shortbread Crust

¾ cup (1½ sticks) unsalted butter, at room temperature

2 cups all-purpose flour

½ cup light brown sugar

½ teaspoon salt

Filling

2 (8-ounce) packages cream cheese, softened

2 large eggs

¾ cup white sugar

1 teaspoon vanilla extract

¾ cup blueberry or other fruit preserves

Topping

16 ounces (2 cups) sour cream (I always use Breakstone)

⅓ cup white sugar

1 teaspoon vanilla extract

I love cheesecake in all forms. This is a great one in the fall also. I use all natural preserves.

Preheat the oven to 350° F.

To make the shortbread base, combine the butter, flour, brown sugar, and salt. Mix by hand until a crumbly dough is formed. Press into 13 by 9-inch baking pan.

Bake for 20 minutes, until golden brown. While the crust bakes, whisk the cream cheese until smooth in a large mixing bowl. Whisk in the eggs, sugar, and vanilla.

Evenly spread the preserves over the hot shortbread and pour the cream cheese mixture over it.

Bake for about 30 minutes, until slightly puffed. Cool completely in the pan and cut into 24 bars.

For the topping, mix the sour cream, sugar, and vanilla together and evenly distribute on top of the completely cooled cheesecake. Bake for 3 to 5 minutes, until set. Serve cold. ❧

BRIDES, BLOSSOMS, AND BUFFETS

WHEN I STARTED DOING WEDDINGS YEARS AND YEARS AGO, I MET WITH THE BRIDE AND THE MOTHER-OF-THE-BRIDE TO PLAN EVERYTHING. But, to me, fathers were and still are the most important part of a wedding because they write the big checks. Now, though, couples are older when they get married, and I find that grooms (no matter who is paying the bill) want to be in on everything. I do small weddings and very elaborate ones, and they are all equally important to me. I cater every wedding reception as if I were doing it for my own daughter. But the weddings that are the most gratifying to me personally are the ones I do for girls who I first saw in the hospital when they were born. So there is a lot of history with some of my brides. Weddings elicit more emotion than any other type of party I do; I spend a lot of time reassuring everyone involved and some time refereeing, usually between daughters and mothers.

When I meet with brides we toss around a lot of ideas. When Katherine Tatum was getting married (She was one of the ones I went to see the day she was born, and now she has a baby!), we were talking about a seafood table in the center of the sculpture garden at the Telfair Art Museum, where the reception was to be held. I said, "Katherine, wouldn't it be great if we had some live goldfish in the center of the table?" So we did. I had a three-foot-high base tightly covered with red roses. Then I put my giant apothecary jar on top of the rose-covered platform into which I put a huge black fish and two huge goldfish. With spotlights on the fish, it was the most dramatic thing you have ever seen and looked spectacular with the black tablecloths and lamps with red shades on the dinner tables.

Two of my most beautiful weddings were in South Carolina. The Morrison wedding reception was held in the dreamy romantic ruins of Old Sheldon Church in Garden's Corner. The chapel, built ca. 1751 for Prince William Parish, was named for the nearby Bull family

plantation, Sheldon Hall. The church burned twice, first when British troops torched it in 1779 during the Revolutionary War and again in 1864 (after being restored in 1824) by Union troops. Now only the outer walls and four majestic columns remain.

The Long wedding, held at the bride's family place in Bluffton, was another exquisite affair. The reception was

a seated dinner for 250 people in a gigantic tent decorated with blue and white, including tablecloths made of fabric the bride's mother brought from France. This party was planned to the nth degree to assure that nothing could go wrong. The decorations and food were perfect, the band was great, and everybody was on the dance floor when I looked out there and saw the bride's aunt dancing up a storm with one very oddly dressed man who definitely stood out among all the tuxedos. He was obviously a crasher, but no one seemed to care. I discreetly asked around until someone told me, "Oh, he's the guy that just brought the pizzas to the band." There are so many crazy things that happen behind the scenes, you just never know.

If someone wants to do something I think is inappropriate for whatever reason, I just tell them that I've been in business for a long time and have a good reputation, and I'm just not comfortable with it. That

always works. For example, I would never have one of those Champagne fountains. I also don't mix my food with someone else's. If a client asks if her Aunt Bessie can make the salad, I politely tell her my business and reputation rests on the food I serve, so I have this policy I have never broken. My last caveat is no paper or plastic plates, glasses, or utensils, even on a boat!

Weddings are the most fun, but I also do big debutante balls and gala fundraisers. These parties are in museums, tents, private clubs, and special settings that local people know about, such as the Arsenal in Beaufort. The Beaufort

Ball, held there before the Museum moved in, was a fundraiser for the Beaufort Museum. We had cocktails in the courtyard, where backlit Gothic arches infused the atmosphere with a mystical feeling as if we were in Xanadu.

The last kind of event I want to mention is one I do often, but rarely talk about—funerals. When someone I know dies, whether they are my clients or not, I take the family chicken pot pies, the best comfort food I know. Often someone in the family will call and ask me to do a buffet at home before or after the funeral. I serve cocktail party food, and, in Savannah, there is usually a well-stocked bar. Even those without a drop of Irish blood seem to know instinctively how to have a good Irish wake. When I go to France, home to Dothan, or to my sister's house in Bridge Hampton, the last thing I always say

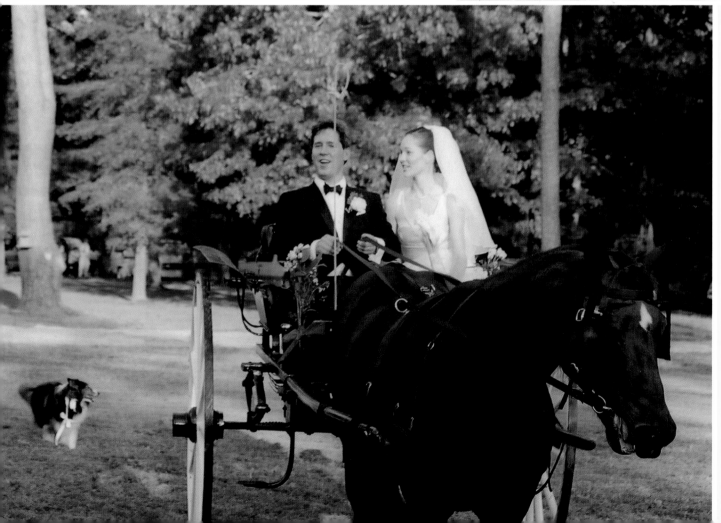

to my staff when I leave is that they can have the whole time off while I'm gone as long as no one dies. A whole lot of praying for the people of Savannah to stay healthy goes on when I'm away.

As Willie Nelson observed, life is full of circles and cycles, phases and stages. The best thing about my career as a caterer is that it allows me to help families mark those phases and stages with memorable events: christenings and baby-namings, bar and bat mitzvahs, family reunions, graduations, deb parties, weddings, special birthdays, and yes, funerals, too. The day this manuscript went to the publisher, I received the following note from Ashley Peeples Oberlin:

Dear Susan,
It occurred to me the other day that the special events in my life—my debutante reception, my wedding, and the christening of my twin sons—have been accompanied by delicious food created by you. Thank you.
Best, Ashley

Thank you, Ashley, for allowing me to be part of the circles and cycles of your life. ✐

Recipes

Jane's Salad

Serves 10

Jane Long, to whom this book is dedicated, is a great friend and a great cook. I catered her daughter's wedding at her summer house in Bluffton, and Jane invented this salad for the wedding dinner. I'm happy to say the wedding was beautiful and our friendship of thirty years survived our working together on Jane's vision of the perfect wedding!

Salad Dressing

½ CUP VEGETABLE OIL

¼ CUP EXTRA VIRGIN OLIVE OIL

¼ CUP APPLE CIDER VINEGAR

1 TEASPOON GARLIC SALT

SCANT TEASPOON SALT

FRESHLY GROUND BLACK PEPPER

1 TEASPOON SUGAR

1 TABLESPOON KETCHUP

1 OUNCE SALT PORK

1 (16-OUNCE) BAG FROZEN BUTTER BEANS OR LIMA BEANS
(I USE MCKENZIE PETITE BUTTER BEANS)

1 ½ POUNDS OKRA, ENDS TRIMMED

8 OUNCES GRAPE TOMATOES OR RED TOMATOES, HALVED AND SEEDED

1 MEDIUM RED ONION, HALVED AND SLIVERED

½ CUP CRUMBLED SAGA CHEESE

8 SLICES BACON, COOKED AND CHOPPED

To make the dressing, combine the oils, vinegar, garlic salt, salt, black pepper to taste, sugar, and ketchup in a jar and shake.

To make the salad, bring 4 cups of water to a boil in a medium saucepan. Add the salt pork and simmer for 20 minutes to flavor the water. Remove the pork. Add the beans and simmer for 10 minutes. Add the okra to butter beans and cook for 2 to 3 minutes. Drain well.

Combine the beans, okra, tomatoes, and onion in a bowl. Toss with the dressing just before serving. Sprinkle the crumbled Saga cheese and bacon over the top. Serve cold or at room temperature.

Potato and Corn Salad with Buttermilk Dressing

Serves 6

Buttermilk Dressing
½ cup BUTTERMILK
2 TABLESPOONS MAYONNAISE
1 TABLESPOON WHITE WINE VINEGAR

12 NEW POTATOES
6 EARS FRESH YELLOW CORN
¼ CUP SALAD OIL
¼ CUP (½ STICK) UNSALTED BUTTER
4 WHOLE SPRING ONIONS (SCALLIONS), TRIMMED
AND CHOPPED

This is so good in the summer when corn is fresh. I use yellow corn and plate it up on radicchio leaves for a lively presentation.

To prepare the dressing, whisk together the buttermilk, mayonnaise, and vinegar in a small bowl. Cover and refrigerate until chilled through, about 30 minutes.

Put the potatoes into a large pot, cover with water, and boil for 20 to 30 minutes, until fork tender. Allow to cool slightly, then peel and slice.

Scrape the kernels from the corn cobs. In a skillet, heat the oil and butter over medium heat. Add the corn kernels and sauté for 6 to 8 minutes, until bright yellow.

Combine the potatoes, corn, and spring onions in a large bowl. Allow to cool, then toss gently with the dressing. Cover and refrigerate for at least 2 hours before serving cold. ❧

Corn Pudding

Serves 6

3 (10-ounce) bags frozen corn, yellow and white
¼ cup all-purpose flour
1 tablespoon sugar
1 teaspoon salt
¼ teaspoon black pepper
⅛ teaspoon of cayenne pepper
2 cups whipping cream
¼ cup (½ stick) butter, melted
3 large eggs, well beaten

This dish is requested often. I like to cook the pudding until it is almost done and then stuff it into hollowed-out tomatoes. The tomatoes are baked at 350° F for about 15 minutes, or until the tomatoes are done but still firm.

Preheat the oven to 350° F. Grease a 1 ½-quart baking dish.

Cut the kernels from the ears of corn. Puree half of the corn in a blender for 4 seconds. Combine the pureed corn with whole corn kernels in large bowl. Add the flour, sugar, salt, pepper, and cayenne and mix well. Mix in the cream, butter, and eggs. Pour into the prepared baking dish. Set the baking dish into a larger pan; fill the larger pan with hot water to a depth on 1 inch.

Bake, uncovered, for about 70 minutes, or until a toothpick inserted in center comes out clean. Serve hot. ✑

Sautéed Scallops

Serves 6

I prepare scallops in a very simple manner because they are very delicate, and I want to get their full flavor. I put these on skewers and pass around at cocktail parties with a saffron mayonnaise. They are also delicious just on a bed of lettuce on their own.

½ teaspoon saffron threads
1 tablespoon hot water
½ cup mayonnaise
1 clove garlic, crushed
1 tablespoon chopped fresh flat-leaf parsley
Salt and freshly ground black pepper
½ cup (1 stick) unsalted butter
18 sea scallops, cleaned (remove the small muscle on the side)

First make the saffron mayonnaise. Steep the saffron in the hot water for 5 minutes in a small bowl. Mix in the mayonnaise, garlic, and parsley. Season to taste with salt and pepper. Chill overnight before serving.

Melt the butter in a large heavy skillet over medium-high heat. Add the scallops in batches and sauté until all are done (2 to 3 minutes per side). The scallops will change color and tighten up when they are cooked. Do not overcook. Drain the scallops, place on a tray, and set aside for 5 to 10 minutes.

Serve the scallops warm with the saffron mayonnaise. ❧

Creamed Oysters

Serves 10 to 12

Oysters and elegance go hand-in-hand, whether the oysters are on a half shell, on a bed of rock salt, or my favorite, served as creamed oysters. I'll often sprinkle fried bacon on top. These don't last long in a chafing dish at a party.

¼ cup (½ stick) butter

2 tablespoons finely chopped onion

¼ cup all-purpose flour

2 cups whipping cream

3 tablespoons chopped fresh chives

2 teaspoons Worcestershire sauce

1 teaspoon salt

1 teaspoon freshly ground black pepper

4 cups shucked oysters (preferably small)

2 tablespoons vegetable oil

Melt the butter in a medium saucepan over medium-high heat. Add the onion and sauté for 2 minutes until limp. Add the flour, stirring for 3 minutes to incorporate. Add the whipping cream and stir until smooth. Add the chives, Worcestershire sauce, salt, and pepper. Cook for a few minutes more.

Drain the oysters. Pick through carefully to remove any shells. Heat the oil in a 12-inch skillet over medium-high heat. Add the oysters and sauté for a few minutes until the edges curl. Then add the oysters to the white sauce. Serve hot. ༅

Lamb Curry

Serves 6

½ cup (1 stick) butter, clarified
2½ to 3 pounds lean lamb, cut into small dice, or about 2 pounds roasted leg of lamb
¼ cup (½ stick) butter
1 large onion, chopped
1 clove garlic, minced
1 teaspoon curry powder
¼ teaspoon salt
¼ cup all-purpose flour
2 cups chicken broth
Toasted coconut, chopped peanuts, chutney, chopped hard-cooked egg, to garnish

This is easy to prepare and can be made ahead and reheated. It is great served over rice.

Heat the clarified butter in a large skillet over medium heat. Add the lamb and sauté until browned. Or dice the roast of leg of lamb and reserve.

In a large saucepan, melt the butter over medium heat. Add the onion and sauté for about 5 minutes until limp. Add the garlic and sauté for 3 minutes. Add the curry powder and salt and sauté until thoroughly mixed. Stir in the flour and cook for 2 minutes, stirring well. Whisk in the stock, and cook until thickened. Add the lamb, bring to a simmer, cover, and cook very gently until the lamb is tender, about 10 minutes.

Serve the curry hot, passing each one of the garnishes in a separate dish. ⤳

Note: To clarify butter, heat in a saucepan over low heat. Do not stir. After the butter melts, skim off foamy layer and discard. Use yellow layer only.

Harriet's Oven Cooked Rice

Serves 10 to 12

1 cup converted rice, rinsed in a colander under cold water
2 cups chicken broth

Harriet Ballenger taught me to make this rice when I lived in Spartanburg, South Carolina, twenty years ago. It comes out perfectly every time and you do not have to watch the pot.

Preheat the oven to 400° F.

Spread the rice in a 13 by 9-inch baking dish. Bring the broth to a boil and pour over rice. Double wrap the baking dish in aluminum foil, wrapping tightly from the bottom and top.

Bake for 1 hour. Serve hot. ⤳

Chicken and Artichoke Casserole

Serves 4 to 6

4 pounds chicken breast, bone in

1 cup (2 sticks) unsalted butter

½ cup all-purpose flour

3½ cups milk

3 ounces Swiss cheese, grated

2 ounces cheddar cheese, grated

—— 1 teaspoon cayenne pepper

1 (8-ounce) jar button mushrooms, drained

2 (14-ounce) cans artichoke hearts, drained

test w/ ½ teaspoon cayenne

This is a great make-ahead meal and easy to assemble. I serve this with white or wild rice.

Bring a large pot of salted water to a boil. Add the chicken and simmer until cooked through, about 20 minutes. Remove the meat from bones. Cut the meat into bite-size pieces. Discard the skin and bones.

Preheat the oven to 350° F. Grease a 13 by 9-inch baking dish.

Melt the butter in a large saucepan over medium heat. Whisk in the flour to make a smooth paste. Slowly add the milk, stirring constantly. Add the cheeses and red pepper. Stir until the cheeses are melted and the sauce is bubbling. (The sauce will not be very thick.) Mix in the chicken, mushrooms, and artichokes. Pour into the prepared baking dish.

Bake for 30 minutes. Serve hot. This casserole freezes well for up to 1 month. ⮞

Marinated Shrimp and Artichokes

Serves 8 to 10

The snow peas and tomatoes add great color. This looks very pretty in a glass bowl. Plus it tastes great.

3 POUNDS SHRIMP, PEELED AND DEVEINED

1½ CUPS TARRAGON VINEGAR

2 TABLESPOONS FRESH LEMON JUICE

1 TABLESPOON LIGHT BROWN SUGAR

1½ TEASPOONS DIJON MUSTARD

1 ONION, QUARTERED

2 CLOVES GARLIC, PRESSED

SALT AND FRESHLY GROUND BLACK PEPPER

4 CUPS VEGETABLE OIL

2 (14-OUNCE) CANS ARTICHOKE HEARTS, DRAINED

8 OUNCES SNOW PEAS

1 PINT CHERRY TOMATOES, HALVED

2 POUNDS MUSHROOMS, SLICED IN HALF

Bring a large pot of salted water to a boil. Add the shrimp, stir, and reduce the heat. Simmer until the shrimp turn pink, about 3 minutes.

To make the marinade, combine the vinegar, lemon juice, brown sugar, mustard, onion, and garlic in a large bowl. Season with salt and pepper. Slowly add the oil, whisking until fully incorporated. Add the shrimp and artichokes. Let marinate overnight in the refrigerator.

To blanch the snow peas, bring water to a boil and throw in snow peas. Cook until bright green, about 2 minutes. Then put the snow peas in cold water to stop the cooking process.

Before serving, add the cherry tomatoes, snow peas, and mushrooms. ✐

Asian Grilled Quail

Serves 8

I don't know why, but men love this dish. If I just use the breast, I put them on skewers and pass around with the sauce in a bowl in the middle of the tray.

¼ CUP HOISIN SAUCE

3 TABLESPOONS CHINESE CHILI SAUCE WITH GARLIC

3 TABLESPOONS DARK SESAME OIL

3 TABLESPOONS HONEY

2 TABLESPOONS SESAME SEEDS

1 TEASPOON GROUND GINGER

8 QUAIL, DRESSED, OR 16 QUAIL BREASTS

1 (14-OUNCE) CAN CHICKEN BROTH

2 TEASPOONS CORNSTARCH

In a large bowl, combine the hoisin sauce, chili sauce, sesame oil, honey, sesame seeds, and ginger. Add the quail, turning to coat. Cover and refrigerate for 30 minutes.

Meanwhile, prepare a medium-hot fire in a gas or charcoal grill.

Remove the quail from the marinade and reserve the marinade. Grill the quail for 30 minutes or until done, turning once.

Pour the reserved marinade into a medium saucepan. Pour ¼ cup of the chicken broth into a small bowl and pour the remainder into the saucepan. Bring contents of saucepan to a boil over medium heat. Meanwhile whisk the cornstarch into the reserved broth until smooth. Then whisk this mixture into the marinade and continue to cook until thickened, about 1 minute.

Serve the sauce with the quail. ❧

CATERING TIPS ❧ ROSE TABLECLOTH

I ALWAYS SAY THAT IT TAKES SIX GIRLS AND SIX BOTTLES OF WINE TO MAKE THIS FABULOUS PIECE! THIS IS A WONDERFUL PROJECT FOR FRIENDS OF THE BRIDE'S MOTHER TO DO FOR THE BRIDE ON THE DAY OF HER WEDDING.

Begin by cutting a circle out of white burlap that is 90 inches in diameter, big enough for a table that stands 4 feet high. Then cover the table with the cloth, place the round cake tray you'll be using in the center, and use it to draw a circle. Now you're ready to take the cloth off the table and spread it out on a tarpaulin.

Starting at the center of the tablecloth, apply the roses in circles as you move outward. You'll need to dip the roses in hot glue pans (like cast-iron skillets) that hold big blocks of melted glue. Four people working at a fast pace can apply 3,000 to 4,000 roses in about 3 hours.

WHITE BURLAP, 90 INCHES LONG
4 FOOT TABLE
CAKE TRAY—SIZE VARIES DEPENDING ON CAKE SIZE
TARPAULIN
HOT GLUE
3 CAST-IRON SKILLETS (FOR GLUE)
10 POUNDS HOT GLUE CHIPS
800 OSIANA ROSES
60 BUNCHES OF PORCELINO ROSES (40 TO 60 ROSES PER BUNCH)

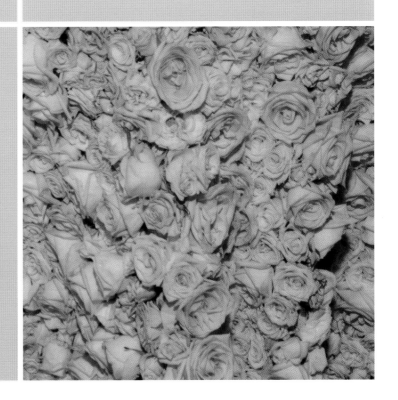

Dothan Marinated Beef Tenderloin

Serves 10 to 12

2 (1-pint) bottles Kraft Zesty Italian Dressing
2 onions, thinly sliced
½ cup sliced pimientos
2 cloves garlic, chopped
1 tablespoon chopped fresh parsley
1 teaspoon salt
½ teaspoon freshly ground black pepper
4- to 5-pound beef tenderloin, oven-ready (trimmed but not tied)

When I was growing up in Dothan, Alabama, this was a dish served at the Dothan Country Club. This is great served on French bread rounds.

Prepare the marinade by mixing together the Italian dressing, onions, pimientos, garlic, parsley, salt, and pepper in large nonreactive bowl.

Roast the tenderloin at 400° F for 20 minutes on each side, until an instant-thermometer registers 120° F, which is rare. Let cool, slice to desired thickness (¼ inch if making sandwiches), and put in marinade. Cover and refrigerate overnight. Serve cold.

Rosemary Roasted Salmon

Serves 4 to 6

2 large bunches fresh rosemary
1 large red onion, thinly sliced
2-pound center-cut salmon fillet with skin
Salt and freshly ground black pepper
2 large lemons, thinly sliced
½ cup extra virgin olive oil

If you want an easy dish for a dinner, this is it. I don't recommend it for the middle of summer because a 500° F oven can heat up a house quickly, and your guests may faint before they see the beautiful finished results.

Preheat the oven to 500° F.

Arrange half of the rosemary in the center of heavy baking dish. Arrange half of the onion on top of the rosemary and place the salmon, skin-side down, in the dish. Add salt and pepper and cover with the remaining onion and rosemary. Place the lemon over the top and drizzle with oil.

Roast for 20 minutes, until flakey or to an internal temperature of 130° F. Serve hot.

Lemon Sorbet in Lemon Shells

Serves 6 to 8

2 CUPS WATER

1 CUP SUGAR

½ CUP FRESH LEMON JUICE

ZEST OF 1 LEMON, GRATED

3 TO 4 LEMONS, FOR SERVING

I serve this to clear the palate between courses. I often place it in lemon shells and serve it on dessert plates.

Combine the water and sugar in a small saucepan and bring to a boil. Lower the heat and simmer until the sugar is dissolved. Remove from the heat. Add the lemon juice and zest.

Pour into a food processor and blend until smooth. Pour the mixture into a glass bowl, cover with plastic wrap, and freeze. Stir once while it is freezing to keep the lemon juice from settling at the bottom.

Core the lemons and scoop each serving of sorbet into half of a lemon shell. Serve immediately. ๛

Creole Pecan Praline Bars

Makes 32 bars or 64 bite-size pieces

Shortbread Layer
½ cup (1 stick) unsalted butter, at
room temperature
1 cup firmly packed light brown sugar
¼ teaspoon salt
2 cups sifted unbleached all-purpose flour
2½ cups large pecan halves (9 ounces)

Praline Topping
¾ cup (1½ sticks) unsalted butter
⅓ cup firmly packed light brown sugar

A long recipe, but it is very simple to put together and makes a good holiday party sweet. We substitute pecan pieces for halves and that cuts down on the prep time.

Preheat the oven to 350° F and position a rack in the center of the oven.

Turn a 13 by 9-inch baking pan upside down. Press a 17-inch length of foil, shiny side down, onto the pan, shaping it to the sides and corners with your hands. Remove the foil. Run tap water into the pan to wet it all over. Pour out all but about 1 tablespoon of the water, then place the shaped foil in the pan and press it against the bottom and sides to make the foil adhere to the pan.

To make the shortbread layer, beat the butter in a medium bowl with an electric mixer at medium-high speed until soft. Add the brown sugar and salt and beat to mix. Add the flour and beat at low speed for 1 to 2 minutes, until the mixture forms tiny crumbs that hold together when pinched.

Turn out the dough into the prepared pan. Using your fingertips, spread the dough to form an even layer, then press down firmly with the palm of your hand. Place the pecan halves, flat sides down, in one direction—they should be touching each other—to cover the dough.

To make the praline topping, melt the butter and brown sugar in a small saucepan, over high heat. Stir with a wooden spatula until the mixture comes to a rolling boil; continue to stir for 30 seconds. Remove the pan from the heat and pour the caramel over the nuts, coating the entire surface as much as possible.

Bake for 22 minutes, until bubbling.

Transfer to a rack to cool. Refrigerate, covered, the cooled praline bars for at least 1 hour and up to 2 days before slicing.

Pumpkin Swirl Cheesecake

Serves 8 to 10

Crust

2¼ cups graham cracker crumbs
½ cup (1 stick) unsalted butter, melted

Filling

4 (8-ounce) packages cream cheese, softened
1⅓ cups sugar
½ teaspoon ground cinnamon
½ teaspoon ground ginger
¼ teaspoon ground cloves
4 large eggs
¼ cup heavy cream
½ cup canned pumpkin puree

In the autumn, Jerry Polk, the owner of my favorite vegetable and fruit stand, brings pumpkins in all sizes and shapes. Although beautiful to look at and to decorate with, we still use canned pumpkin for our pumpkin cheesecake, because it is available year-round. This is a real crowd-pleaser in any season.

Preheat the oven to 325° F.

To make the crust, combine the graham cracker crumbs with the butter in medium-size bowl. Press the mixture onto the bottom and part of sides of a 9-inch springform pan. Bake the crust for 5 minutes. Remove from the oven and set aside.

Beat the cream cheese in a large mixing bowl on high speed with an electric mixer for 2 to 3 minutes, until creamy.

In a small bowl, mix together the sugar, cinnamon, ginger, and cloves. Add to the cream cheese, beating on medium-high speed for 2 to 3 minutes, until the mixture is smooth and fluffy. Add the eggs, one at a time, beating well with each addition. Add the heavy cream and mix well.

Combine the pumpkin puree in a medium mixing bowl with 1 cup of the cream cheese mixture. Pour the remaining cream cheese mixture into the prepared crust. Spoon 6 large dollops of the pumpkin mixture evenly over the cream cheese mixture. Use the back of the spoon to gently swirl the pumpkin through the batter to form orange streaks. Be careful not to touch the bottom crust.

Place the cake in the center of the oven and bake until the cake is set, about 1¼ hours. Remove from the oven, let cool slightly, then refrigerate overnight. Unlock side of pan and lift off, leaving the cake on bottom. Serve on bottom pan. ⇘

INDEX

Additional photo credits:

Richard Leo Johnson: p.117 *(left)*, p.134-135

SCAD Campus Photography Archives: p.65 *(top right)*,
    p.84, p.117 *(right)*, p.120, p.150, p.151